SHAKESPEARE
The Writer and his Work

To the Reader.

This *Figure*, that thou here feeſt put,
    It was for gentle *Shakeſpeare* cut;
Wherein the *Graver* had a ſtrife
    With *Nature*, to out-doe the *Life* :
O, could he but have drawn his *Wit*
    As well in *Braſſe*, as he has hit
His *Face* ; the *Print* would then ſurpaſſe
    All, that was ever writ in *Braſſe*.
But ſince he cannot, *Reader*, look
    Not on his *Picture*, but his *Book*.

B. J.

William Shakespeare: engraving by Martin Droeshout for the title page of the
First Folio, 1623, with Ben Jonson's commendatory verses.
Mansell Collection, London

SHAKESPEARE

The Writer and his Work

by

STANLEY WELLS

CHARLES SCRIBNER'S SONS
NEW YORK

COVER
The Chandos Portrait: oil painting by an unknown artist.
National Portrait Gallery

CONTENTS

Quotations and references are taken from
The Complete Works, ed. P. Alexander, 1951.

SHAKESPEARE

I. STRATFORD AND LONDON

WILLIAM SHAKESPEARE was baptized in the great church of Holy Trinity, Stratford-upon-Avon, on 26 April 1564. Probably he was born no more than two or three days previously; 23 April, St George's Day, traditionally celebrated as the date of his birth, is as likely to be correct as any. At the time his father was an up-and-coming young man who took a prominent part in administering the town's affairs. He had married Mary Arden, who came from a family of higher social standing, about 1552, the year in which he was fined 12d. for failing to remove a dunghill from outside his house. For years after this, as his children were born and, some of them, grew up, his position among his fellow-townsmen improved. He was a member of the glovers' guild, and also dealt in wool and, probably, other commodities. In 1556 he was appointed an ale-taster, with responsibility for the price and quality of the bread and ale offered to the town's two thousand or so inhabitants. He moved upwards in the hierarchy: as constable (1558), principal burgess (about 1559), chamberlain (1561), alderman (1565), and, in 1568, bailiff, or mayor, and justice of the peace.

At this high point in his career he was the father of two sons, William and Gilbert (1566–1612). Two daughters, Joan and Margaret, had died in infancy. Another Joan was born in 1569; a Richard born in 1574 lived, apparently in Stratford and a bachelor, till 1613; and a late child, Edmund, came in 1580; he became an actor in London, and died early, aged twenty-seven.

When young William was four years old, he could have had the excitement of seeing his father, dressed in furred scarlet robes and wearing the aldermanic thumb-ring, regularly attended by two mace-bearing sergeants in buff, presiding at fairs and markets. Perhaps a little later, he would have begun to attend a 'petty school' to acquire the rudiments of an education which would be furthered at the King's New School. We have no lists of the pupils at this time, but his father's position would have qualified him to attend, and the education offered was such as lies behind the plays and poems. The school had a well qualified master, with the relatively good salary of £20 a year, from which he had to spare £4 to pay an usher, or assistant, to teach the younger boys. At the age of about eight Shakespeare would have begun a regime which might well have sent him 'unwillingly' on the quarter-of-a-mile walk from his father's Henley Street house to the schoolroom above the Guildhall and next to the Guild Chapel. Classes began in the early morning, and hours were long. The basic medium of instruction was Latin. A charming scene in *The Merry Wives of Windsor* (IV.i), hardly required by the plot, shows a schoolmaster instructing young boys in their grammar, and must be an amused recollection of the dramatist's own schooldays. From grammar the pupils progressed to rhetoric and logic, and to works of classical literature. They might read *Aesop's Fables* and the fairly easy plays of Terence and Plautus, on one of which Shakespeare was to base an early comedy. They might even act scenes from them. They would go on to Caesar, Cicero, Virgil, Horace, and Ovid, who was clearly a favourite with Shakespeare in both the original and Arthur Golding's translation published in 1567.

But there was a life beyond school. Shakespeare lived in a beautiful and fertile part of the country; the river and fields were at hand; he could enjoy country pursuits. He had younger brothers and sisters to play with. Each Sunday the family would go to church, where his father as bailiff and, later, deputy bailiff, sat in the front pew as his rank required. There he would hear the sonorous phrases of the Bible, in either the Bishops' or the Geneva version, the Homilies, and the Book of Common Prayer, all of which made a lasting impression on him, as well as lengthy sermons that may have been less memorable. Sometimes groups of travelling players came to Stratford. Shakespeare's father would have the duty of licensing them to perform, and probably the boy saw his first plays in the Guildhall immediately below his schoolroom.

As he grew into adolescence, his father's fortunes waned. John Shakespeare fell into debt, and after 1576 stopped

The master bedroom of John Shakespeare's house in Henley Street, Stratford, in which William Shakespeare is said to have been born. *Holte Photographics*

attending council meetings. His fellows treated him leniently, but in 1586 felt obliged to replace him as alderman. In 1592 he was listed among those persistently failing to go to church, perhaps for fear of arrest for debt.

But by this time William was in London, already displaying the genius which would enable him to recoup the family fortune. How he kept himself after leaving school we do not know. In 1582, at the age of eighteen, he married Anne Hathaway of Shottery, a mile or so from his home. The marriage was hasty, the bride, eight years older than her husband, pregnant. The clerk of the Worcester court to which application for a special licence was made on 27 November wrote her name, mistakenly, it seems, as Anne Whateley of Temple Grafton. A daughter, Susanna, was baptized in Holy Trinity on 27 May 1583, and twins, Hamnet and Judith, on 2 February 1585.

The seven years that follow are a blank in our knowledge. Shakespeare may, as Aubrey reported a century later, have become a 'schoolmaster in the country'. He may have followed one or more of the innumerable other avocations—

9

The King Edward VI Grammar School, Stratford: the schoolroom interior.
British Tourist Authority

lawyer, soldier, sailor, actor, printer—that have been foisted upon him. He may have travelled overseas. All we know is that at some point he left Stratford, joined a theatrical company, went to London, and began to write—not necessarily in that order. The first certain printed allusion to him shows that, as actor turned playwright, he had aroused the envy of the dying Robert Greene who, in 1592, wrote scornfully of an 'upstart crow' who thought himself 'the only Shakescene in a country.' Parodying a line from *3 Henry VI*, Greene conveniently helps to establish a date by which that play was written. His malice provoked a defence of Shakespeare by a minor playwright, Henry Chettle, who wrote of him as one whose 'demeanour' was 'no less civil than he excellent in the quality he professes. Besides, divers of worship have reported his uprightness of dealing, which argues his honesty, and his facetious grace in writing, which approves his art.' Evidently he was well established in London by this time. But apparently he lived always in lodgings there, setting up no household. He seems to have felt that his roots were in Stratford. His family stayed there. How often he visited them we cannot tell. He had no more children. Perhaps he was gradually able to help his father who, in 1596, applied successfully for a grant of arms, and so became a gentleman. In August of the same year, William's son, Hamnet, died. In October, William was lodging in Bishopsgate, London, but in the next year he showed that he looked on Stratford as his permanent home by buying a large house, New Place, next to the Guild Chapel and the Grammar School.

Over the following years, his growing worldly success can be followed in both Stratford and London records. In 1598 a minor writer, Francis Meres, published a book called *Palladis Tamia: Wit's Treasury*, which includes the passage: 'As Plautus and Seneca are accounted the best for comedy and tragedy among the Latins, so Shakespeare among the English is the most excellent in both kinds for the stage; for comedy, witness his *Gentlemen of Verona*, his *Errors*, his *Love Labour's Lost*, his *Love Labour's Won*, his *Midsummer's Night Dream* and his *Merchant of Venice*: for tragedy, his *Richard II*, *Richard III*, *Henry IV*, *King John*, *Titus Andronicus* and his *Romeo and Juliet*.' We do not know what he meant by *Love Labour's Won*. It may be a lost play, or an alternative title for a surviving one. The main importance of the list is that it gives us a date by which all these plays had been written. Add to it the two narrative poems, the three parts of *Henry VI*, *The Taming of the Shrew*, and (perhaps) the sonnets, and it is a remarkable output for a man of thirty-four, especially one who is usually regarded as a late starter.

In October 1598 Richard Quiney, whose son was to marry Shakespeare's daughter Judith, went to London to plead with the Privy Council on behalf of Stratford Corporation, in difficulties because of fires and bad weather. He wrote a letter, never delivered, to Shakespeare asking for the loan of £30, a sum large enough to suggest confidence in his friend's prosperity. In 1601 Shakespeare's father died. In May of the following year he paid £327 for 127 acres of land in Old Stratford. In 1604 he was lodging in London with a Huguenot family called Mountjoy, and became mildly involved with their daughter's marital problems. In the same year, through a lawyer, he sued for recovery of a small debt in Stratford. In 1605 he paid £440 for an interest

Hewland Farm, now known as Anne Hathaway's Cottage, the home of the Hathaway family in Shakespeare's time.   *British Tourist Authority*

in the Stratford tithes. In June 1607 his daughter Susanna married a distinguished physician, John Hall, in Stratford; his only grandchild, Elizabeth, was christened the following February. In 1609 his mother died there.

About 1610, Shakespeare's increasing involvement with Stratford suggests that he was withdrawing from his London responsibilities and retiring to New Place. He was only forty-six years old, an age at which a healthy man was no more likely to retire then than now. Probably he had a physical breakdown. If so, it was not totally disabling. He was in London in 1612 for the lawsuit from which we know of his involvement with the Mountjoys. In March 1613 he bought a house in the Blackfriars for £140; he seems to have regarded it rather as an investment than as a domicile. In the same year, the last of his three brothers died. In late 1614 and 1615 he was involved in disputes about the enclosure of the land whose tithes he owned. In February 1616 his second daughter, Judith, married Thomas Quiney, causing William to make alterations to the draft of his will, which was signed on 25 March. By now, surely, he knew that he was mortally ill. He died, according to his monument, on 23 April, and was buried in a prominent position in the chancel of Holy Trinity Church.

This selection of historical records shows clearly that Shakespeare's life is at least as well documented as those of most of his contemporaries who did not belong to great families. The identification of the Stratford worthy with the world's playwright is confirmed, if any confirmation is necessary, by the inscription on the memorial in the parish church, erected by 1623, which links him with Socrates and Virgil, and by much in the far greater memorial of that year, the First Folio edition of his plays, in which his great contemporary and rival, Ben Jonson, calls him 'Sweet Swan of Avon'.

II. SHAKESPEARE'S INTELLECTUAL AND THEATRICAL BACKGROUND

For a poetic dramatist, Shakespeare was born at the right time. He grew up during a period of increasing stability and prosperity in England. Queen Elizabeth was unifying the nation. Patriotic sentiment was increasing. Continental influences were helping in the transmission of classical knowledge which we call the Renaissance. The arts in general were flourishing; those of literature and drama bounded forward far more rapidly than in the earlier part of the century. The years between Shakespeare's birth and his emergence in London saw the appearance of the first major translations of Ovid, Apuleius, Horace, Heliodorus, Plutarch, Homer, Seneca, and Virgil; Shakespeare seems to have known most of these, and those of Ovid and Plutarch, at least, had a profound influence on him. During the same period appeared William Painter's *Palace of Pleasure*, an important collection of tales including some by Boccaccio which Shakespeare used; Holinshed's *Chronicles*; Lyly's *Euphues*; Sidney's *Arcadia* and *Astrophil and Stella*; early books of Spenser's *Faerie Queene*; Lodge's *Rosalynde*; prose romances and other pamphlets of Robert Greene; the early writings of Thomas Nashe; and other books which Shakespeare either used or must have known. Indeed, it is no exaggeration to say that almost all Shakespeare's major sources are in books written or first translated into English during the first thirty years of his life, though of course he could have read the Latin works, and, probably, those in French and Italian, even if they had not been translated. The greatest earlier English author known to him was Chaucer, and he was considerably influenced by the publication in 1603 of Florio's translation of Montaigne's *Essays*.

English dramatic literature developed greatly in Shakespeare's early years. Four years before his birth, blank verse was introduced as a dramatic medium in Sackville and Norton's *Gorboduc*. When he was two years old, George Gascoigne's *Supposes*, a translation from Ariosto and the first play written entirely in English prose, was acted; he was to draw on it in *The Taming of the Shrew*. These are early landmarks. He was already a young man before the pace of development really accelerated. John Lyly's courtly comedies, mostly in prose, began to appear in 1584, the year in which George Peele's *The Arraignment of Paris* was presented to the Queen. The pace increased in the later 1580s, with Kyd's *The Spanish Tragedy*, Greene's *James IV*, and, above all, the emergence of Christopher Marlowe. Shakespeare was finding his feet in the theatre. Our knowledge of the exact ordering of events in this period is so uncertain that we cannot always say whether he is influenced by the writers of these plays or himself exerts influence on them. What is undeniable is that English drama was rapidly increasing in range, scope, and power. Prose was for the first time becoming a rich dramatic medium, all the more so for its intermingling with verse styles which were immeasurably enriched by the ever more flexible uses that writers were making of blank verse. Growth in the size of acting companies and in the popularity of theatrical entertainment

The Swan Theatre, Bankside. An early copy of a drawing by Johannes de Witt who visited the theatre in 1596. This is our only detailed picture of an Elizabethan theatre interior. *Mansell Collection, London*

tectum

porticus

sedilia

orchestra

ingressus

mimorum aedes

proscænium

planities sive arena

...untium sed spari et structura, bestiarum conflictati ni destinatum, in quo multi ursi, tauri, et stupenda agnitudinis canes, distinctis cautis et septis aluntur; qui sui

S. PAULES CHURCH

the water house

Quene hythe

Three Cranes

The Eell Schipes

The Gally fuste

THAMESIS

The Bear Gardne

The Globe

encouraged the writing of more ambitious plays, interweaving plot with sub-plot, tragedy with comedy, diversified with songs, dances, masques, and spectacular effects in ways that were unknown only a few years before.

The rapid progress of dramatic literature was thus inextricably linked with equally important developments in the theatrical arts. Shakespeare was twelve when James Burbage, already the father of the boy who was to become the greatest actor of Shakespeare's company, erected the Theatre, the first building in England designed primarily for theatrical performances. Before this, acting companies had roamed the land, the better ones under noble protection, playing where they could—in halls of great houses, Inns of Court, guildhalls, inn-yards. Now one company, at least, had a permanent building; it was followed by others. The companies grew in size. They had the facilities to perform increasingly ambitious plays. They were encouraged by enthusiastic audiences and by the pleasure taken in drama by the Queen and her Court, even though they had also to resist the opposition of Puritan forces. They were, at the least, highly competent. Some gained international reputations. Boy actors, progressing through a system of apprenticeship, played female roles in a fully professional manner.

The Elizabethan theatre, with its open roof, thrust, uncurtained stage, absence of representational scenery, rear opening, and upper level, was a sophisticated, if fundamentally simple, instrument. Modern theatre designers are returning with excitement to its basic principles. It could accommodate spectacle and machinery, yet many plays written for it could be performed also in the unequipped halls that companies had to use on tour. It was a non-representational, emblematic medium, shaped by and shaping the poetic dramas which prevailed on its stages.

We do not know when Shakespeare joined a company of players. In 1587 the Queen's Men lost one of their actors through manslaughter in Oxfordshire. They visited Stratford soon afterwards. That they there enlisted Shakespeare is no more than an intriguing speculation. Some evidence suggests that he may have belonged to Pembroke's Men, first heard of in 1592. Certainly he was one of the Lord Chamberlain's

Panoramic view from J. C. Visscher's map of London, c. 1616: the true positions of *The Globe* and *The Bear Garden* have been reversed. *Mansell Collection, London*

Men shortly after they were founded, in 1594, and remained with them throughout his career. Rapidly this became London's leading company, outshining its main rival, the Lord Admiral's Men, led by Edward Alleyn. With the Chamberlain's Men, Shakespeare became a complete man of the theatre: actor, business-man, and dramatic poet. He is the only leading playwright of his time to have had so stable a relationship with a single company. He wrote with their actors specifically in mind, and the conditions in which they performed helped too to shape his plays. They flourished, built the Globe as their London base from 1599, survived the competition of the successful children's companies in the early years of the new century, acquired King James I as their patron in 1603, soon after his accession, increased in size while remaining relatively stable in membership, and by 1609 were using the Blackfriars as a winter house—a 'private' theatre, enclosed, smaller, more exclusive in its patronage than the Globe. Perhaps it affected Shakespeare's playwriting style: yet his plays continued to be performed at the Globe, and elsewhere.

III. EARLY SHAKESPEARE

The beginnings of Shakespeare's career as a writer are obscure. We have no juvenilia, sketches, or drafts. Yet beginnings there must have been. Even his earliest plays demonstrate a verbal power that suggests a practised writer. Problems of chronology bedevil attempts to study his development. Regrettably, the editors of the First Folio did not print the plays in order of composition, but imposed on them an arrangement into kinds: comedies, histories, and tragedies. The divisions are imperfect. Some of the tragedies are historical; some of the histories are tragical; and Shakespeare's greatest comic character appears in one of the histories. Shakespeare was no neo-classical respecter of the limits of dramatic genres. By reference to external evidence, such as contemporary allusions, and internal evidence, mainly stylistic development, scholars have attempted to determine the order of the plays' composition. The chronology proposed by E. K. Chambers is still accepted, with slight modification, as orthodox; but it remains partially conjectural. To treat the works in the assumed order of their composition would suggest more certainty about this order than is justified. To adopt the Folio's grouping would risk losing all sense of Shakespeare's development. In these pages, the works will be divided into four groups: those written by about 1594, then those written between about 1594 and 1600, 1600 and 1607, and 1607 and 1612. Within these divisions, the plays will be grouped by genre.

Early Histories

One of the earliest theatrical projects in which Shakespeare was engaged was also one of the most ambitious: to transfer to the stage Edward Hall's narrative, in the last part of *The Union of the Two Noble and Illustre Families of Lancaster and York* (1548), of events, spanning over fifty years, which led to the founding of the Tudor dynasty in the marriage of Henry VII to Elizabeth of York. The resulting plays were printed in the First Folio as *1, 2* and *3 Henry VI* and *Richard III*. The first three seem to have been written by 1592, when Greene alluded to a line from the third. Bad texts of the second and third appeared in 1594 and 1595 respectively, as *The First Part of the Contention betwixt the Two Famous Houses of York and Lancaster* and *The True Tragedy of Richard, Duke of York*. It has often been doubted whether *1 Henry VI* is entirely by Shakespeare. He may have revised someone else's work in order to form a dramatic sequence, but the plays are so closely related to one another that they are easily conceived of as the product of a single mind.

The enormous cast lists of the *Henry VI* plays reflect the difficulty of concentrating and focusing the mass of historical material. Some of the exposition of dynastic issues is laboured, some of the action sketchily represented. Shakespeare's powers of individual characterization through language were not yet fully developed, and in Henry VI he was saddled with the liability of a passive hero. Perhaps in deference to decorum, Parts One and Three are composed entirely in verse; it does not avoid monotony. And some of the theatrical conventions employed are very much of their time, as the direction 'Enter the KING with a supplication, and the QUEEN with Suffolk's head' (Part Two, IV. iv) is enough to show.

Nevertheless, these plays have many merits. They examine England's past in the light of its present at a time of national self-consciousness, of pride in national unity and fear that it might be dissipated, as Henry V's had been. On the way, they entertain and teach. They also display a deeply serious concern with political problems: the responsibilities of a king, his relationship with his people, the need for national unity, the relationship between national welfare and self-interest, the suffering caused by dissension, whether between nations or opposing factions within a nation, often mirrored in the image of a family, royal or not.

These concerns are bodied forth with much artistic success in the dramatic form and style. Part One, for example, opens with masterly thematic appropriateness in its portrayal of the ritual of national and personal mourning over the body of Henry V, nobly expressed, but rapidly degenerating into a family squabble. The scene ends with Winchester's declaration of personal ambition, just as the play ends with similar sentiments from Suffolk:

> Margaret shall now be Queen, and rule the King;
> But I will rule both her, the King, and realm.

Though the poetic style of these plays is often formal and declamatory, with extended similes and frequent classical allusions, there are also vivid, deflationary moments of colloquialism, as when Joan of Arc answers the enumeration of Talbot's honours with:

> Him that thou magnifi'st with all these titles,
> Stinking and fly-blown lies here at our feet.
> (Part One, IV.vii. 75–6)

Part Two has some excellent prose. The scenes of Cade's rebellion show at an early stage Shakespeare's capacity for serious comedy. The horrifying episode in which Cade comments on the severed heads of Say and Cromer (IV.iii) justifies this Senecan device, because it combines with situation and language to provide an entirely convincing representation of the savagery of mob rule.

At times Shakespeare withdraws from the hurly-burly of violent action into reflective scenes of great beauty. The pastoral ideal is expressed as well as anywhere in the remarkable scene of the Battle of Towton (Part Three, II.v), which, for all its stylization, forms a perfect dramatic emblem of the personal consequences of war. Henry, dismissed from the battle as useless, envies the shepherd's life. To one side of him appears a son carrying the body of a man he has killed, whom he discovers to be his father; to the other, a father carrying the body of a man he has killed, whom he discovers to be his son. Henry joins in their grief, and adds his own:

> Was ever King so griev'd for subjects' woe?
> Much is your sorrow; mine ten times so much.

Many of the most powerful scenes in these plays are of mourning, especially of children and parents. Yet the plays are memorable also for their portrayal of energetic evil, sometimes in figures of amoral wit, even charm. Especially remarkable are the Duke of York's sons: Edward, later King Edward IV; George, Duke of Clarence; and Richard, Duke of Gloucester. Richard grows rapidly in menace in Part Three, emerging as the complete anti-hero in the splendid soliloquy in which he declares his ambitions:

> I'll drown more sailors than the mermaid shall;
> I'll slay more gazers than the basilisk;
> I'll play the orator as well as Nestor,
> Deceive more slily than Ulysses could,
> And, like a Sinon, take another Troy.
> I can add colours to the chameleon,
> Change shapes with Protheus for advantages,
> And set the murderous Machiavel to school.
> Can I do this, and cannot get a crown?
> Tut, were it farther off, I'll pluck it down.
>
> (III.ii. 186–195)

The rhetorical patterning, the end-stopped lines, the classical allusions, often regarded as limitations of Shakespeare's early style, contribute to a wonderfully energetic portrayal of the flights of Richard's imagination, which leads naturally to his dominance in *Richard III*. This play, of which a bad quarto appeared in 1597, cannot have been written much later than its precursors, but in it Shakespeare creates from his chronicle sources an aesthetically and morally satisfying pattern that shows him as the complete master of his material, able to subdue the world of fact to that of art.

Again, family relationships are important. Richard's engineering of Clarence's murder is ironically contrasted with their elder brother Edward's death-bed efforts to re-unite the family. Richard bustles his way to the throne, over-coming all obstacles in a gloriously entertaining display of cynical hypocrisy, intelligence, and wit. But the forces of retribution grow in strength, and are especially associated with women's mourning for the victims of past crimes. Murders of innocent children are seen in these plays as ulti-mate crimes against humanity. Richard's downfall begins when he alienates his chief supporter, Buckingham, by ask-ing him to arrange the murder of his young nephews, the princes in the Tower. Tyrrel's description of their deaths (IV.iii) is an emotional climax. Opposition to Richard is focussed in the idealized figure of Richmond, and the grand climax to the ritual of this and all these plays comes as the ghosts of Richard's victims appear to him and to Richmond. Richard's waking soliloquy shows that his self-sufficiency has defeated itself:

> I shall despair. There is no creature loves me;
> And if I die no soul will pity me:
> And wherefore should they, since that I myself
> Find in myself no pity to myself?
>
> (V.iii. 200–203)

He dies fighting, and Richmond's closing speech restates the image of England as a family:

> England hath long been mad, and scarr'd herself;
> The brother blindly shed the brother's blood,
> The father rashly slaughter'd his own son,
> The son, compell'd, been butcher to the sire.

Now he, as Henry VII, and Elizabeth, heirs of the houses of Lancaster and York, will bring unity to the kingdom. This patriotic climax, spoken by Elizabeth's grandfather, must have been peculiarly satisfying to the plays' first audiences.

Shakespeare is also concerned with dynastic issues in *King John*, a play about an earlier period of English history, first printed in 1623 but apparently written in the early 1590s. It is based in part on *The Troublesome Reign of John, King of England*, printed anonymously in 1591. As in the *Henry VI* plays, there is a strong sense of the futility and wastefulness of war. Shakespeare portrays a conflict in which neither side is right. King John knows that his claim to the English throne is weak. The French king, Philip, withdraws his support of the rival claimant, Prince Arthur, when John offers to make an advantageous match between his niece and the French Dauphin. On both sides, selfishness, scheming, and personal greed put 'commodity'—self-interest—before the common good. Shakespeare treats the situation ironically in, for instance, the scene before Angiers (II.i). The French Herald calls on the citizens to admit Arthur

> Who by the hand of France this day hath made
> Much work for tears in many an English mother,
> Whose sons lie scattered on the bleeding ground.
>
> (ll. 302–4)

The English Herald immediately calls on them to admit John and his soldiers,

> all with purpled hands,
> Dy'd in the dying slaughter of their foes.
>
> (ll. 322–3)

The blood of both sides is wasted, for neither has won. There is a farcical element in the impasse, and in John's acquiescence in the suggestion that the opposing armies should unite to

> lay this Angiers even with the ground;
>   Then after fight who shall be king of it.
>
> (ll. 399–400)

The ironical attitude finds personal embodiment in the figure of the Bastard, Philip Faulconbridge, who serves for the first half of the play as an ironic commentator. But grief is important here, too. Prince Arthur's mother, Constance, gives powerful expression to suffering and loss, and Arthur's threatened blinding and his death form an emotional focus. The discovery of his body turns the Bastard from a commentator into a participant, committed to humanity and England's welfare; and he ends the play as his country's spokesman:

> This England never did, nor never shall,
> Lie at the proud foot of a conqueror,
> But when it first did help to wound itself. . . .   ·
> Come the three corners of the world in arms,
> And we shall shock them. Nought shall make us rue,
> If England to itself do rest but true.

Early Comedies

The mode of the history play was new when Shakespeare began to work in it; he may even have originated it. Comedy, however, had a long ancestry, and his early plays in this kind draw heavily on traditional modes and conventions, as if he were consciously experimenting, learning his craft by a process that included both imitation and innovation.

The Two Gentlemen of Verona, not printed till 1623, is clearly an early play. It derives partly from the prose romances popular in the late sixteenth century. The simple plot comes, perhaps indirectly, from a Portuguese romance, *Diana*, by Jorge de Montemayor. Shakespeare's craftsmanship in shaping it for the stage often falters. The play reveals his limited capacity at this period to orchestrate dialogue. Thirteen of its twenty scenes rely exclusively upon soliloquy, duologue, and the aside as comment. Scenes requiring the

24

ability to show a number of characters talking together are generally unsuccessful. Most of the characters are only two-dimensional; some are laughably unrealized.

But *The Two Gentlemen of Verona* is full of charm and promise. It uses many motifs that Shakespeare was to develop in later plays. Those episodes in which he works within his limitations are often entirely successful. An example is the delightful scene (IV.ii) in which Proteus serenades his new love with 'Who is Silvia?', while his old love looks on in disguise. The ironic word-play of Julia's dialogue with the Host suggests real depth of character. Valentine and Proteus, too, have some human substance; and Proteus's servant, Launce, is the first in the great line of Shakespearian clowns. His monologues are masterpieces of comic dramatic prose, constructed with an artistry consummate enough to give the impression of artlessness. Some of the verse, too, is masterly; witness the astonishing matching of sound to sense in Proteus's tribute to the power of poetry:

> For Orpheus' lute was strung with poets' sinews,
> Whose golden touch could soften steel and stones,
> Make tigers tame, and huge leviathans
> Forsake unsounded deeps to dance on sands.
>
> (III.ii. 78–81)

The Two Gentlemen of Verona shows Shakespeare as already a great writer, though not a great playwright.

The Comedy of Errors, also first printed in 1623, was written by Christmas 1594, when it was played at Gray's Inn. Its dramatic economy is much superior to that of *The Two Gentlemen of Verona*. Here, Shakespeare draws heavily on the traditions of Roman comedy. The action takes place in Ephesus within a single day, and is based on Plautus's farce *Menaechmi*, which tells of a man accompanied by his slave and in search of his long-lost twin brother. Shakespeare turns the slave into a servant, Dromio, and gives him, too, a twin, who serves his master Antipholus's brother. The identical twins have identical names, and the result is a great increase in the possible errors of identification. Shakespeare frames the classically derived main action within an episode based on the romantic story of the wanderings of Apollonius of

Tyre, which he was to use again in *Pericles*. This gives the Antipholuses a father, Egeon, and the comic complexities of the main action are overshadowed by his being condemned to die at five o'clock unless he can find someone to redeem him. By this and other means Shakespeare interfuses what might have been a merely mechanical farce with pointers to the potentially serious consequences of the misunderstandings. The untying of the comic knot is preceded by a moving lament from Egeon, about to be executed, who is not recognized by the man he believes to be the son he has brought up from birth. The resolution is effected by an Abbess who turns out to be Egeon's wife, a surprise to the audience paralleled in Shakespeare's work only by the apparent resurrection of Hermione, in *The Winter's Tale*.

The ending of *The Comedy of Errors* is not just a solution of an intellectual puzzle, it is charged with emotional power. This play is a kind of diploma piece. In it Shakespeare outdoes his classical progenitors. He adapts his style admirably to his material. He modifies the intellectual complexity of his plot by infusing romantic motifs into it, and by relaxing the pace of the action from time to time to allow for the inclusion of discursive set-pieces such as Dromio of Syracuse's marvellous prose description of the kitchen-wench who was 'spherical, like a globe.' There is no faltering here.

The Taming of the Shrew, printed in the Folio, has a problematic relative, a play printed in 1594 as *The Taming of A Shrew*, once looked on as Shakespeare's source, now more generally regarded as a corrupt text of his play. It includes a rounding off of the Christopher Sly framework which corresponds with nothing in the Folio. Perhaps that text is damaged, too. Editors and directors sometimes, justifiably, add these episodes to the Folio text on the grounds that they may derive from lost Shakespearian originals.

In *The Comedy of Errors*, Shakespeare shows people losing their sense of identity when recognition is withheld from them, and acquiring a sense of reaffirmed identity when normality returns. In the Induction to *The Taming of the Shrew*, he suggests how changes in external circumstances may join with the power of rhetoric to create a sense of changed identity. This play draws partly on conventions of

Roman comedy, partly on English folk tale and drama. It owes a distinct debt to *Supposes*, George Gascoigne's prose translation of Ariosto's *I Suppositi*. 'Supposes' is as much a key-word in *The Taming of the Shrew* as is 'errors' in *The Comedy of Errors*. The Induction displays the trick by which Sly is made to suppose that he is not a tinker but 'a mighty lord.' In the play performed for Sly's amusement, Lucentio, wooing Bianca, employs various 'counterfeit supposes', but they are superficial. He, the shallowly romantic lover, is opposed to the unromantic Petruchio, who comes

> to wive it wealthily in Padua;
> If wealthily, then happily in Padua. (I.ii. 73–4)

Petruchio is offered Kate, the shrew, apparently a far less attractive match than Bianca. And the most vital part of the play demonstrates the 'suppose' by which he transforms the shrew into the ideal wife. The process is partly physical, partly mental. But its effect is not to reduce Kate to a state of subjection. Rather it teaches her the importance in human relationships of the ability to participate imaginatively in other people's lives. The play's final scene derives warmth and joy from the fact that Kate, in her new relationship with Petruchio, feels a freedom and wholeness that were previously outside her grasp. The achievement of Petruchio the realist is a romantic one: he creates an illusion and turns it into reality.

The Taming of the Shrew is a robust play that acts splendidly. It shows Shakespeare experimenting with techniques of structure and language in order to integrate a variety of diverse materials. It is interesting in the critical attitude that it adopts to romantic conventions. It contains much fine verse and prose; but, in the surviving text, it lacks the subordination of all the parts to the whole which causes a less ambitious play, such as *The Comedy of Errors*, to seem a more rounded work of art.

Love's Labour's Lost is so different as to remind us forcibly of the uncertainties in the chronology of the early plays. Here Shakespeare seems to be writing for a more sophisticated, even courtly audience. The influences of earlier comedy appear to have been filtered through the plays of

John Lyly, the leading Court dramatist. The play contains topical allusions, some no longer explicable, which may also suggest that it originally had a coterie audience. It was first published in 1598, 'as it was presented before her Highness this last Christmas', when it was said to be 'newly corrected and augmented.' But it was also acted in the public theatres—according to the title page of the second quarto, of 1631, 'at the Blackfriars and the Globe'—and a Court performance of 1605 suggests that it was not purely topical in its appeal.

In this play Shakespeare employs an exceptionally wide range of verse and prose styles, demonstrating his command of verbal artifice. This is appropriate, for the play is much concerned with artificiality. The King and his three lords have imposed unnatural restrictions on themselves. Beside them Shakespeare places Holofernes, the pedant who stands as an awful warning of what they may become if they persist in their denial of nature, and Costard and Jaquenetta, unspoilt children of nature. The arrival of the Princess of France and her three ladies offers an immediate challenge to the lords' resolutions, and the play's patterned, dance-like progress charts their slow acceptance of their own natures, their acknowledgments of the demands of society and the need for a proper and courteous use of the intelligence. Artificial behaviour is reflected in artificial language. Significantly, the most important communication in the play does not need to be put into words:

> *Marcade*   . . . the news I bring
>   Is heavy in my tongue. The King your father—
> *Princess*
>   Dead, for my life!
> *Marcade*   Even so; my tale is told.   (V.ii. 706–9)

Artifice gives way before the ultimate reality of death. The lovers are forced into new relationships with one another, and Shakespeare shows that the adjustment is not easy.

The subdued ending of *Love's Labour's Lost* represents one of Shakespeare's most daring experiments with comic form. Usually, the comic climax brings happiness; this one brings grief. After it comes a slow movement towards resignation and hope, but the happy ending lies in the future, at least twelve months away; and that, says Berowne, is 'too long for a play'. *Love's Labour's Lost* offers its audience full enjoyment of artifice, but also invites a critical attitude towards it. The play grows from intellectual playfulness to a warm humanity which comes to full, disturbing flood at the close. It is a play of ideas, a brilliantly dramatized debate; though in some senses it is of its age, it can still reach out vividly to us.

Shakespeare's early experiments in comedy have their perfect outcome in *A Midsummer Night's Dream*, printed in 1600 but probably written by 1595. No single influence is dominant. The design of the play came from Shakespeare's imagination, as it had for *Love's Labour's Lost*, with which it has much in common. It too has a patterned structure, a wide range of prose and verse styles, comedy springing from the follies of young love, a play-within-the-play. It has a similar grace of language, less intricacy and self-conscious brilliance. The theory that it was written for an aristocratic marriage is unsupported by external evidence, but marriage is central to the play's design, linking each of the distinct groups of characters. Theseus is to be married; the lovers wish to be, and finally are; the fairies, who have marital problems, are to intervene in the human plans for marriage, and to deliver the concluding epithalamium; the labourers are to provide the entertainment for the multiple marriages, and one of them is bemusedly to receive the amorous attention of the Fairy Queen.

Though marriages form the natural conclusion to the action, there are, in the usual way of comedy, obstacles to be overcome. Misunderstandings among the young lovers are exacerbated by Puck's mischief; dissension between the Fairy King and Queen must be settled before human happiness can be achieved. The supernatural world is lightly suggestive of inexplicable influences upon human behaviour, especially in love—'reason and love keep little company together now-a-days.' And Shakespeare is led to explore the relationship between reason and the imagination in a way that suggests an affinity between love and artistic responsiveness. The inexperienced lovers are bewildered by their own emotions. The labourers are hopelessly confused by the problem of distinguishing between appearance and reality. But the lovers, temporarily released from the bands of society, come out of the dream world of the wood wiser than they had gone into it. Bottom is taken out of himself by his encounter with the Fairy Queen and, though he regards it as a dream, acknowledges it as 'a most rare vision'. Theseus looks with the eye of reason, but Hippolyta knows that

> all the story of the night told over,
> And all their minds transfigur'd so together,
> More witnesseth than fancy's images,
> And grows to something of great constancy.
> (V.i. 23–26)

The last act is a glorious celebration, a dance in which the shifting relationships between the performers of the interlude, the images they try to present, and their audience mirror the conflicting claims of illusion and reality, the world of the imagination—in which openness to experience can lead to wisdom—and the need to acknowledge the hard facts of life. The performance ends in goodwill and courtesy, on which the fairies bestow their blessing; and Puck, in his closing lines, reminds us that we are at liberty to take what we have seen as either truth or illusion:

> If we shadows have offended,
> Think but this, and all is mended,
> That you have but slumb'red here
> While these visions did appear.

The goodwill of the audience can help the players to 'mend'. As Holofernes had shown, imaginative detachment is 'not generous, not gentle, not humble'; and, as we had witnessed in *The Taming of the Shrew*, imagination can turn illusion into reality.

Early Tragedies

Shakespeare was more tentative in his early explorations of tragic than of comic form. Tragedies were conventionally based on history, and *Titus Andronicus* is set in the fourth century A.D., but the story, like that of his other early

30   A scene from *Titus Andronicus* showing Tamora pleading for her sons going to execution. A sketch possibly drawn by Henry Peacham 1576?–1643?: the only illustration to a Shakespeare play which has survived from his time. *By permission of the Marquis of Bath: photograph by courtesy of the Courtauld Institute of Art*

Titus... the complete gentleman

Tamira
pleadinge

Enter Tamora pleadinge for her sonnes
going to execution

Tam: Stay Romane bretheren gratious Conquerors
Victorious Titus rue the teares I shed
A mothers teares in passion of her sonnes
And if thy sonnes were ever deare to thee
Oh thinke my sonnes to bee as deare to mee
Sufficeth not that wee are brought to Roome
To beautifie thy triumphes and returne
Captive to thee and to thy Romane yoake
But must my sonnes be slaughtered in the streetes
for valiant doinges in there Cuntryes cause
Oh if to fight for kinge and Common weale
Were piety in thine it is in these
Andronicus staine not thy tombe wth blood
Wilt thou drawe neere the nature off the Gode
Drawe neere them then in being mercifull
Sweete mercy is nobilityes true badge
Thrice noble Titus spare my first borne sonne

Titus: Patient your self madame for dye hee must
Alarbus do you likewise prepare your self

Aron: And now at last repent your wicked life
If now I curse the day and yet I thinke
few comes within the compasse off my curse
Wherein I did not some notorious ill
As kill a man or els devise his death
Ravish a mayde or plott the way to do it
Accuse some innocent and forsweare my selfe
Sett deadly enmity between two freindes
Make poore mens cattell breake theire neckes
Sett fire on barnes and hay stackes in the night
And bid the owners quench them wth theire teares
Oft have I digd up dead men from their graves
And sett them upright at their deere freindes dore
Even almost when theire sorrowes was forgott
And on theire breste as on the barke off trees
Have with my knife carved in Romane letters
Let not your sorrow dye though I am dead
Tut I have done a thousand dreadfull thinges
As willingly as one would kill a fly
And nothing greves mee hartily indeede
But that I cannot do ten thousand more &c.

so far
from
statius
Titus
Andronicus
Sc. 2

Henricus Peacham
Anno mo qqto

tragedy, *Romeo and Juliet*, is fictitious. Shakespeare may have adapted it from an earlier version of *The History of Titus Andronicus*, which survives only as an eighteenth-century chapbook. Ovid, whose *Metamorphoses* appears on stage (IV.i), is an important influence, as is Seneca. Except for Act Three Scene Two, which first appeared in print in 1623, the play was printed in 1594, and it may have been written several years earlier, perhaps in collaboration with George Peele, perhaps merely under his influence. Popular in its time, it can now be enjoyed only with an exercise of the historical imagination, for its presentation of physical horror can easily seem ludicrous. The disjunction between action and language can bewilder, as when Marcus, seeing his niece with 'her hands cut off, and her tongue cut out, and ravish'd' (II.iv), delivers nearly fifty lines of beautifully modulated blank verse; or, still more surprisingly, when Titus, having persuaded Aaron to cut off his hand, betrays no more emotion in what he says than if he had taken off a glove. Nevertheless, it is in the portrayal of suffering that the play justifies itself, and more than one production has shown that, given the right kind of stylized presentation, its ritualistic tableaux of suffering and woe can be profoundly moving. As in the early histories, Shakespeare is most successful in the expression of grief and the portrayal of energetic evil. Titus's lament over his mutilated daughter is elemental in a way that looks forward to Lear:

> I am the sea; hark how her sighs do blow.
> She is the weeping welkin, I the earth;
> Then must my sea be moved with her sighs;
> Then must my earth with her continual tears
> Become a deluge, overflow'd and drown'd.
> (III.i. 226–230)

Aaron, the Moorish villain, displays an enjoyment of evil and a cynical intelligence that relate him to Richard III and Iago; he develops into the play's most complex character. The final horrifying bloodbath, in which Titus serves Tamora with her two sons' heads baked in a pie, kills his own daughter and Tamora, and is himself killed by the Emperor, who is then killed by Titus's son, is skilfully engineered, but the events are efficiently rather than imaginatively presented, and tragic emotions are not stirred.

Shakespeare took the well-known story of Romeo and Juliet from Arthur Brooke's long poem *The Tragical History of Romeus and Juliet*, published in 1562 and reprinted in 1587. The play is more markedly experimental than *Titus Andronicus*. It is not set in antiquity, but in the sixteenth century. It has affinities with romantic comedy, telling of wooing and marriage. Its poetical centre is the balcony scene, perhaps the most celebrated expression of romantic love in our literature; the romance is offset by much witty and bawdy comedy. The tragic outcome of the lovers' passion is the result of external circumstances: the still timelessness of Romeo and Juliet's inward experience, perfectly conveyed at the end of the balcony scene, is threatened and finally destroyed by the time-tied processes of the public feud between their families. The play, first printed in 1597, seems from its verbal styles to have been written several years after *Titus Andronicus*. For the first time among the plays discussed so far, we feel, not merely that the design is ambitious, but that Shakespeare's fecundity overflows the measure. Every rift is laden with ore, and the finished work delights and astonishes by its inventiveness, variety, complexity, and generosity. But it is not undisciplined. Indeed, this play is 'early' in the sense that it still relies partly on formal verse structures—the lovers' first conversation, a moment of private communion in the public bustle of the ball, is cast in the form of a sonnet—and on clearly patterned action. Public strife is counterbalanced by private communion; the Prince, the civic governor, has his counterpart in Friar Lawrence, the personal confessor; Romeo's confidant, Mercutio, is matched by Juliet's, her Nurse. Characterization is both brilliant and functional. Shakespeare's verbal virtuosity makes marvellous individuals out of Mercutio and the Nurse, but they too are part of the pattern, each failing one of the lovers in understanding, pushing them still further into isolation. In their bawdy physicality, too, they act as foils to the lovers, whose passion includes but transcends the physical. Romeo and Juliet are gradually destroyed by the world of external reality: the world of uncomprehending relatives and friends, in which the senseless family feud—a symbol of misunderstanding, of the failures in human communication—destroys the most precious representatives of the families. Romeo and Juliet had achieved understanding and union; they had risked—and, in a sense, lost—all for the values of personal love. In this sense comedy is banished from the end of the play. The Prince calls together the heads of the opposing families and speaks of general woe. But out of the suffering comes a hard-won reconciliation. As in some of Shakespeare's later comedies, the union of lovers accompanies the healing of breaches among members of the older generation; but here, the lovers are dead.

The Poems

Because of plague, London's theatres were closed for almost two years between June 1592 and June 1594. Shakespeare turned to non-dramatic writing, perhaps because he feared that he might need an alternative career. A new kind of narrative poem was coming into vogue: tales of love based on Ovidian stories and techniques. Thomas Lodge's *Scilla's Metamorphosis* (1589) is an early example. Another, perhaps the finest, is Christopher Marlowe's *Hero and Leander*. Marlowe died in 1593, but the poem was not published till 1598. *Venus and Adonis* was printed in 1593, with the author's dedication to Henry Wriothesley, Earl of Southampton, calling the poem 'the first heir of my invention'—presumably meaning either his first poem or his first work to be printed. It was extraordinarily popular; at least eleven editions appeared before 1620, and five more by 1640. Partly it had a *succès-de-scandale*; Shakespeare makes Venus the suitor, Adonis her reluctant victim, which adds a piquant eroticism to Ovid's story.

The poem's success has not been maintained. Like *Love's Labour's Lost*, it is a sophisticated work, drawing attention to its craftsmanship, demanding admiration rather than submission. It will not be enjoyed if it is read for its story alone: Shakespeare takes nearly 1200 lines where Ovid took about 75. Yet the narrative is unfolded with such order, clarity, and

The Earl of Southampton: oil painting by John de Critz the Elder, c.1601.
The portrait shows Southampton during his imprisonment in the Tower
after Essex's unsuccessful uprising. *The Duke of Buccleuch and Queensberry*

ease of versification that the general impression is one of speed. The style, though artificial, is varied, ranging from metaphysical elaboration to pared simplicity. Adonis provides the main psychological interest. His innocence and idealism contrast with Venus's experience and paradoxically physical, materialist outlook. It is the goddess who represents lust, the human boy who stands up for love. The tension between his youthful withdrawal from sexual experience and her over-mature anxiety to rush into it provides the poem's dramatic impetus. Adonis's immaturity, amusing and touching, is appropriate to the essentially non-tragic nature of a story with a quasi-tragic ending.

The Rape of Lucrece, printed the following year, and also dedicated, more warmly, to Southampton, is a contrasting companion piece. The earlier poem is mythological. *Lucrece*, composed in the seven-line rhyme royal, is historical, based not on the *Metamorphoses* but on the *Fasti* ('Chronicles'). It is about people in society; its tone is not that of high comedy, but of tragedy. Like *Venus and Adonis*, it opens with speed in a stanza that carries concentrated suggestions of the power of Tarquin's lust. A long poem could not be sustained at this pitch, nor would the slender story support it. Shakespeare ekes out his material with meditative soliloquies, discursive episodes, and long moralizing passages. The amplificatory technique is less successful here than in *Venus and Adonis*. There, we could remain detached enough to enjoy the poet's verbal flights, his decorative ingenuity, his digressive skill. *Lucrece* seems to demand more engagement with the emotions of the characters. Even the least relevant passages are often fine in their own right, but the parts are greater than the whole. Most important from the point of view of Shakespeare's later development seem to be those passages describing how Tarquin against his better nature is drawn inexorably on towards the crime that will destroy him. Just as a basic theme of Shakespearian comedy, the search for, and final achievement of, self-knowledge, is adumbrated in *Venus and Adonis*, so a basic motif of his tragedies, the problem caused by an absence of self-knowledge so disastrous that it is finally destructive of self, emerges in *Lucrece*. Tarquin, we are told, as he moves towards Lucrece's chamber, 'still pursues his fear' (l. 308). Macbeth, before he kills Duncan, imagines Murder moving 'With Tarquin's ravishing strides, towards his design' (II.i. 55).

It may have been about the time that Shakespeare was writing the essentially public narrative poems that he also wrote his most seemingly private compositions, his sonnets. When they were written is only one of the mysteries about them. In 1598, Francis Meres referred to Shakespeare's 'sugared sonnets among his private friends.' In 1599, William Jaggard published corrupt versions of two of them in *The Passionate Pilgrim*, a volume of poems which he attributed to Shakespeare and which also includes three extracts from *Love's Labour's Lost*, four poems known to be by other poets, and eleven of unknown authorship which few have ascribed to Shakespeare. The complete 154 sonnets did not appear until 1609, though the title-page declaration 'Never before imprinted' implies that they were not new. The publication appears to be unauthorized. It has a dedication by the publisher, Thomas Thorpe: 'To the only begetter of these ensuing sonnets Mr W.H. all happiness and that eternity promised by our ever-living poet wisheth the well-wishing adventurer in setting forth.' This sentence has been endlessly discussed, but we still do not know who Mr W.H. is, nor in what sense he was the sonnets' 'only begetter'. The volume also includes 'A Lover's Complaint', a narrative poem whose authenticity is doubtful.

Sonnet sequences were popular in the 1590s, and Shakespeare's interest in the sonnet form is reflected in some of his early plays, especially *Romeo and Juliet* and *Love's Labour's Lost*. The fact that he did not publish his sonnets may imply that he thought of them as personal poems, but this is not altogether borne out by their content. Some are generalized meditations; some are comparatively formal utterances, like the first seventeen, in which he urges a young man to marry and beget children. Some proclaim a public design in the attempt to eternize their addressee. Some hint at a personal drama. The relationship between the poet and his friend is so close that it is sometimes interpreted as homosexual, though this is explicitly denied (20). It is threatened by another poet who seeks to replace the author in his friend's affections; the

TO.THE.ONLIE.BEGETTER.OF.
THESE.INSVING.SONNETS.
M*r*.W.H. ALL.HAPPINESSE.
AND.THAT.ETERNITIE.
PROMISED.

BY.

OVR.EVER-LIVING.POET.

WISHETH.

THE.WELL-WISHING.
ADVENTVRER.IN.
SETTING.
FORTH.

T.T.

The dedication to The Sonnets, 1609. *Photograph University of London Library* poet's mistress, a 'black woman' (as he calls her), or Dark Lady, seduces the friend: the poet is more concerned for the friend than for his own relationship with the woman, which he frequently deplores. Sonnets 127–152 are mainly about the woman. They include some of the most tortured and introverted of the poems; it is difficult to imagine the poet wishing to show them even to the woman, let alone make them public. This personal drama might be fictional; if so, it is inefficiently projected. The sonnets are partly 'dramatic' in the sense that some of them are written as if from within a particular situation, like speeches from a lost play. Some can be related to classical poetry; some draw on poetic conventions of the time; some represent a deliberate reaction against convention: few if any other sonnets of the time are as bawdy or as insulting to their addressees as some of Shakespeare's. A dramatic poet as great as Shakespeare may have written sonnets on imaginary themes which sound personal, but we know of no reason why he should have done so without intending to publish them. Yet as an autobiographical document, the sonnets are most unsatisfactory. Innumerable attempts have been made to rearrange them into a more coherent sequence, to identify the persons involved, and elucidate topical allusions. None has succeeded.

To read all the sonnets consecutively is difficult. Though almost all of them have, superficially, the same form, this obscures the fact that their wide range of modes, of tone, of variations within the basic form, of intensity, and of interrelationship imposes disparate demands upon the attention. Some, including many of the most popular, are lyrical, confident outpourings of love, conveyed largely through natural imagery; some express the lover's humility and abasement. Some are well ordered meditations on eternal poetic themes of time, the transience of beauty, and of love; on the power of art, the inevitability of death; some are more narrowly, even enigmatically, related to a particular situation. Some are intellectual, witty workings out of poetic conceits; some, no less intellectual, are tortured, introspective self-communings. Though some seem to belong to the world of *The Two Gentlemen of Verona* or *Romeo and Juliet*, others are closer to *Measure for Measure* or *Troilus and Cressida*.

Shakespeare the man remains as fascinatingly enigmatic in the sonnets as in the plays.

IV. LATER HISTORIES AND MAJOR COMEDIES

After his wide-ranging earlier experiments, Shakespeare narrowed his scope and, during several prolific years after about 1594, wrote only comedies and history plays, of which *Richard II* alone is in tragic form. Here Shakespeare steps backward in his dramatization of history to begin a tetralogy which, by carrying the story up to the reign of Henry V, will complete an eight-play sequence. The plays are strongly linked, yet each has its own individuality. *Richard II*, written about 1595, was printed in 1597. It was of topical interest. Queen Elizabeth was ageing. Anxiety about the succession was growing. The Queen's indulgence of her favourites caused unrest; comparisons were drawn between her and Richard II. The absence from the play of the deposition scene (IV.i) in the three editions printed during her lifetime must be attributed to censorship, official or not; and the commissioning by Essex's supporters of a special performance on the eve of his rebellion, in 1601, shows that many drew the parallel.

Nevertheless, Shakespeare's play has no obvious topical allusions. He emphasizes the universal rather than the particular elements of Bolingbroke's usurpation. The play is full of moral ambiguity. Richard, a faulty human being and a weak king, has the unquestioned right to the throne. Bolingbroke has no hereditary right, but is wronged by Richard and better fitted for kingship. Shakespeare skilfully manipulates the audience's sympathies. In the early scenes, we can only condemn Richard's frivolity and irresponsibility, which culminate in his callous and unconstitutional treatment of his dying uncle, John of Gaunt, whose noble speech on England (II.i. 31–68) laments the lapsing values of the old order. But after Bolingbroke becomes king, and also abuses power in the executions of Bushy and Bagot and the arrest of the Bishop of Carlisle—another spokesman for traditional values—and as Richard's expression of his sufferings grows in eloquence, Richard takes on the stature of a tragic hero. Through him Shakespeare orchestrates, in wonderfully melodious verse, all the resonances of the situation, and the play expands from a political drama into an exploration of the sources of power, of the hold that symbols, including words, can have over men's imaginations, of the tensions between the demands of office and the qualities of those who hold office, of private and public values, of the differences and similarities between a 'large kingdom' and a 'little grave'.

Bolingbroke's guilt haunts him throughout the next two plays of the sequence. Carlisle's prophecy that civil war will follow usurpation is fulfilled. *1 Henry IV* (printed twice in 1598 and reprinted five times before 1623) shows the King, wishing to expiate his guilt by a pilgrimage to Jerusalem, anguished by both national and filial rebellion. Just as, in *A Midsummer Night's Dream*, Oberon and Titania must be reconciled before the mortals' course of love can run smooth, so the dissolute Hal must reform and be reconciled with his father before rebellion can be put down. The issue resolves into a personal conflict between Hotspur, the rebel leader, and Hal, who defeats expectation and becomes the victor. Shakespeare has adjusted the facts, chronicled by Holinshed, to create a basically simple foundation on which he builds a history play with a greater social and emotional range than he had so far attempted. Here his genius for character portrayal, achieved largely through an astonishing capacity to deploy and extend the full resources of the English language, is at its greatest. Dominant is Falstaff, Shakespeare's invention, though distantly related to the historical Sir John Oldcastle as portrayed in *The Famous Victories of Henry V*, a minor source play printed in 1598. The character is rich, as the soliloquies particularly demonstrate; but the profundity of the role derives also from its integration into the total design, most subtly in the first tavern scene (II.iv) when Falstaff and Hal in turn take on the role of the King. Behind the game lurks reality, a subconscious and premonitory acknowledgment on Falstaff's part that the 'son of England' should not 'prove a thief and take purses', and on Hal's that he is bound eventually to 'banish plump Jack'. The tavern world provides more fully realized representatives of the ordinary folk of England than we have seen before. It is part of Hal's achievement to link this world with the court and the battlefield.

At the beginning of *2 Henry IV*, Hal seems to have returned to his former ways. There is an uncharacteristic element of repetition in the pattern of paternal reproach, filial repentance, and reconciliation. This may result from an initial uncertainty about whether to treat Henry IV's reign in one play or two. But Part Two has its individual tone, darker and more disturbing than its predecessor's. It brings to the surface moral issues only latent in the earlier play. Even there Falstaff at his most contemptible, stabbing Hotspur's corpse, was juxtaposed with Hal at his most heroic. Here, though we may temporarily condone Falstaff's misuse of his powers of conscription and his exploitation of Shallow and his companions, his self-exculpations are less disarming. In the great tavern scene (II.iv), his amorous exchanges with the deplorable Doll Tearsheet are poignant rather than funny, overshadowed by impotence and the fear of death. But Shakespeare does not encourage us to be morally complacent. Mistress Quickly and even Doll are presented in ways that show his delight in normal human instincts, as well as an awareness that they may be dangerous when out of control. Prince John may have right on his side, but the trick by which he betrays the rebels is distasteful; we can warm to Falstaff's condemnation of 'the sober-blooded boy'. The darker side of tavern life is savagely evident in the tiny scene (V. iv) of Doll's carting—'the man is dead that you and Pistol beat amongst you'. The scene is strategically placed just before Hal's entrance as King; we can see the need for his rejection of Falstaff, though we can see the sadness of it, too.

2 Henry IV was written about 1598. First printed in 1600, it was, unlike Part One, not reprinted till 1623. At this stage in his career, Shakespeare was using a higher proportion of prose over verse than at any other period, and was achieving with it some of his most complex and truly poetical effects.

The political scenes of this play use verse, much of it very fine. But the quintessentially Shakespearian parts are the tavern scene and the Justice Shallow episodes, in which prose is handled with a subtlety matched only in Chekov for the dramatic expression of emotional complexity.

Shakespeare rounded off his second historical sequence with *Henry V*. An apparent allusion to Essex in the Chorus to Act V suggests that it was written in 1599. A corrupt text of the following year omits the Choruses, first printed in 1623. *Henry V*, composed at the zenith of Shakespeare's career as a comic dramatist, brings history close to comic form. It has a wooing scene, and ends, as comedies conventionally do, with a marriage, one that will unite realms as well as hearts (V.ii. 351). Our reactions are guided by the Chorus—Shakespeare's most extended use of this device except in *Pericles*—who speaks some of the play's finest poetry. From the 'civil broils' of the earlier plays, Shakespeare turns to portray a country united in war against France. There is more glory in such a war, and the play is famous—or notorious—as an expression of patriotism. It has less inwardness than its predecessors. But the horrors of war are strongly presented; the goal of war is peace, and the play suggests that inward peace of conscience is necessary in one who would win national peace. Henry shows concern about the justification for his course of action. More than once, and from both sides of the Channel, we are reminded of his 'wilder days'. The transition from 'madcap prince' to the 'mirror of all Christian kings' involves loss. Falstaff is dying; 'the king has killed his heart'. But Henry has accepted the responsibilities of kingship, and talks of them, and its hollow rewards, in a speech that recalls one by his father (*2 Henry IV*, III.i. 1–31) and anticipates (historically) one by his son (*3 Henry VI*, II.v. 1–54). 'The King is but a man' (IV.i. 103), and this one moves among his men with an honesty unimaginable in Richard II and quite different from his father's 'courtship to the common people' (*Richard II*, I.iv. 24). His success in battle removes the guilt of his inheritance. He has become the 'star of England' (final Chorus, 6). If in the process he has made difficult decisions with harsh consequences, that, Shakespeare implies, is the price of political success.

Shakespeare wrote his later histories over the same period as his greatest comedies. *The Merchant of Venice*, dating from about 1596, was entered in the Stationers' Register in 1598 and printed in 1600. Much of the plot material is implausible, deriving from folk tale and legend. The wooing story comes from a collection published in Italian in 1558 as *Il Pecorone*, by Ser Giovanni Fiorentino. The pound-of-flesh story was well known. A lost play, *The Jew*, mentioned in 1579, may have been a source, and Shakespeare must have known Marlowe's *The Jew of Malta*.

The plot's sharp conflict between romantic and anti-romantic values leads Shakespeare to define, partly by contrast, his first great romantic heroine and his first great comic antagonist. The opposition of Portia and Shylock provides the chief dramatic impetus, culminating in the controlled excitement of the trial (IV.i). It is easy to think of the play in terms of contrasts: between the beautiful, generous, merciful Portia and the scheming, miserly, legalistic Shylock; between their religions, Christianity and Judaism; between their settings, the idealized Belmont and the money-markets of Venice; between the heights of lyrical poetry to which Portia can rise, and Shylock's harsh prose. There are other tensions, too: the familiar conflict, in Bassanio, between love and friendship; the opposition, in the episodes of the caskets, between attractive but hollow superficiality and the rewards given to those 'that choose not by the view' (III.ii. 131).

The oppositions in the play, though strong, are not entirely simple. The world of Belmont is idealized but flawed. The generous Bassanio has been prodigal. Antonio, noble in friendship, admits to treating Shylock with contempt. Gratiano, though ebullient, is vindictive. Even Portia has to adopt Shylock's legalism to achieve her good ends. Shylock, though villainous, has dignity, eloquence, and pathos. We may deplore his values yet respect his tenacity. Despite its lyricism, grace, drama, and high comedy, many people find *The Merchant of Venice* disturbing, and express unease with it. Shakespeare portrays here a clash of values rather like that between Henry V and Falstaff. We know which side is right. We have no doubt that Portia should defeat Shylock as King Henry has to reject Falstaff. But in both plays there is pain in the defeat as well as joy in the victory.

Much Ado About Nothing, usually dated about 1598—it is not mentioned by Meres, and was published in quarto in 1600—is also based on a traditional tale. It places less emphasis on poetry and romance, more on prose and wit. The young lovers of the main plot, Claudio and Hero, are unconvincing advocates for romantic values. Admittedly, Claudio expresses his love for Hero eloquently in the play's first verse passage, but only after he has assured himself that she is an heiress. We never see him alone with her, and their relationship seems as insubstantial as that of Lucentio and Bianca in *The Taming of the Shrew*. Claudio falls remarkably easily into the deception that Don John engineers, and gives Hero no opportunity to defend herself before launching into his bitter denunciations at the altar where they were to have been married. Her apparent death leads him to no real soul-searchings, and her forgiveness and their subsequent reconciliation are sketchily presented. Questions are raised that might have been answered if we had more knowledge of Shakespeare's intentions. If Claudio is played as a callow adolescent, we may pity his succumbing to Don John's evil trickery. If he is more maturely presented, we may look on him rather as an illustration of the hollowness of attitudes to love that are based on illusion instead of knowledge and understanding.

Certainly the lovers of the main plot are less convincing than those of the sub-plot. There is more true poetry in single prose sentences of Beatrice's—'There was a star danc'd, and under that was I born'—than in many lines of Claudio's verse. This overturning of expectations is one of the ways in which romantic values are questioned. Beatrice and Benedick's 'merry war', for all its wranglings, suggests a true engagement of personalities. The brief passage in which they declare their love (IV.i. 255-end) is perhaps the best prose love-scene in the language, and we believe in them as complex and developing individuals.

In *Much Ado About Nothing*, recurrent overhearings become a structural principle. 'Nothing' in the title has been taken as a pun on 'noting', and certainly the 'misprisions' arising from the overhearings create the complications of the action. Almost all are tricked. Yet a fruitful counterpoint arises from the relationships of the different sets of characters. Dogberry and his companions of the watch have already overheard Borachio's confession when Claudio denounces Hero. The presence of Beatrice and Benedick during the scene of the thwarted wedding is an additional reassurance to the audience. Dogberry and his fellows are the most naturally befuddled characters, yet it is their basic goodwill that, in spite of almost insuperable barriers to communication, resolves the action. The play's interpretative problems are not essentially different from those of most stage works for which we have limited knowledge of the author's intentions. And they enhance rather than diminish its theatrical robustness. It withstands varied treatments, and is a constant source of pleasure.

There is a legend that Shakespeare wrote *The Merry Wives of Windsor* rapidly, because Queen Elizabeth wanted to see 'Sir John in love.' A passage in Act Five alluding to the ceremony of the Feast of the Knights of the Garter clearly has topical reference, and the play almost certainly has some connexion with special Garter ceremonies, but we cannot be sure in what year. 1597 has been suggested, but the play's relationship with the other Falstaff plays seems to require a later date. It was first published, in a bad text, in 1602; a better text appeared in the Folio. In spite of its superficial naturalism it has a strongly literary background. Several of the characters derive from Shakespeare's own plays about Henry IV, and though no clear source of the plot has been identified, it is closely related to the ribald tales of tricked lovers and husbands included in many contemporary collections.

Legends about the play's origin, and the fact that its central character is called Falstaff, have damaged its critical reputation. It might be more profitably approached as another of Shakespeare's experiments. It is untypical in various ways. It includes proportionally more prose than any other of his

Queen Elizabeth I: oil painting by an unknown artist. *National Portrait Gallery*

plays. It is his only comedy to have an English setting and to be closely related to contemporary life. In Master Ford, Shakespeare comes closer than anywhere else to writing 'humours' comedy in the Jonsonian style. But Shakespeare could never commit himself to Jonson's anti-romantic view of life. Ford is shamed out of his jealous humour, and kneels to his wife for pardon. Falstaff also undergoes a corrective process of castigation leading to penitence. Shakespeare's essential romanticism shows itself too in the sub-plot of Anne Page and her suitors. The climax of the love plot comes in the verse passage in which Fenton, safely married, not merely defends his deception of Anne's parents but rebukes them for their previous opposition to the match and their willingness to have her married for money (V.v. 207–217).

The Merry Wives of Windsor does not belong to the main-stream of Shakespearian comedy, but is recognizably Shakespearian. It is a neat, ingenious, witty comedy of situation. It has attributes of the corrective, satirical comedy that Jonson was making popular at the close of century, but it also displays a strong moral bent and a romantic attitude to love and marriage. The style suits the matter, and much of the writing is delightful, even if it would not be at home in *Henry IV*. The characterization is partly by types, but the major roles offer excellent opportunities to their performers, and there are passages of subtly manipulated dialogue. Critics have patronized the play. Audiences never fail to enjoy it.

Pastoralism, derived from classical models, exerted an important influence on sixteenth-century literature. We have seen how some of Shakespeare's kings envied the shepherd his life attuned to the seasons and the natural processes. Elsewhere, too, Shakespeare plays with pastoral conventions. In *The Two Gentlemen of Verona* and *A Midsummer Night's Dream*, for example, the movement of lovers from their accustomed environment to a place apart assists their self-discovery. But it is in *As You Like It* that Shakespeare conducts his most searching examination of the pastoral ideal. The play, first published in 1623, is based on Thomas Lodge's *Rosalynde*, a prose romance printed in 1590 and reprinted in 1592, 1596, and 1598. Shakespeare's play of the book, written about 1600, is exceptionally literary in its origins, and he does not attempt to conceal its artificiality. He manipulates the relationship between story and dialogue, between the enactment of events and reflection upon the events, between characters as agents of the action and characters as talkers, to permit the introduction of many of the commonplace debating topics of his times: the relationship for instance between nature and fortune, nature and nurture, court and country. These topics are all associated with the pastoral tradition. Related to them is an idea that fascinated Shakespeare: that wisdom is a kind of folly, folly a potential source of wisdom. He seems to have felt that the effort to attain wisdom may result in an over-earnestness that can lead to folly, and that the unguardedness of the subconscious, relaxed mind may, for all its dangers, bring the rewards of unsought illumination. He betrays a concern with the proper use of man's time on earth, and in this comedy in which the central character plays so elaborate, extended, and ultimately important a game, the idea of time, of its uses and abuses, is also, appropriately, pervasive.

Rosalind's game is directed towards the attainment of love, and attitudes to love are dominant among the play's concepts. The forest of Arden is inhabited by lovers, actual and potential. Silvius and Phebe are straight out of the Renaissance pastoral convention, unreal but touching, because in them Shakespeare isolates one aspect of love. Opposed to it is the earthy love affair of Touchstone and Audrey. Touchstone's attitude is partly a criticism of Silvius's, but is itself criticized: being purely physical, it is, as he perceives himself, temporary. Subsuming both of these attitudes is that of Orlando and Rosalind. Orlando has attributes of the conventional lover. He hangs verses on trees, sighs out his soul in praise of his beloved. Yet his idealism is robust enough to withstand the mockery of Jaques, the professed cynic, whose criticism is seen to be destructive, joyless, self-absorbed and without love.

The fullest character of the play, the one who embraces most attitudes within herself and resolves them into a rich synthesis of personality, is Rosalind. Aware of the humorous aspects of love, she knows its potency, too. Her awareness of the danger of folly becomes a self-awareness born of experience, her boyish disguise a means of simultaneously revealing and controlling her emotion. She bears secrets; her revelation that she is a woman is an inward as well as an outward resolution of the play's action. In an early scene, Amiens congratulates Duke Senior on being able to 'translate the stubbornness of fortune / Into so quiet and so sweet a style' (II.i. 19–20). The quality of human experience is determined partly by the character of the experiencer; Jaques will always be melancholy, but Rosalind and Orlando can win quietness and sweetness from adversity by an exercise of the imagination. To this extent, life can be as we like it.

As You Like It gains its impetus rather from the juxtaposition of opposed attitudes than from plot tension. In *Twelfth Night*, also written about 1600 and not published until 1623, Shakespeare returns to a tighter structure. Part of the plot is based on a story from Barnaby Rich's *Farewell to Military Profession* (1581), but Shakespeare idealizes its characters and heightens its romantic tone. The romance framework of separation, search and reunion that he had already used in *The Comedy of Errors* is here more closely integrated into the action, and there is only one pair of twins to cause comic complications. As in *As You Like It*, love is a unifying motif, but it is often a wistful, frustrated, and sometimes non-sexual emotion. The play opens with Orsino's richly romantic expression of thwarted passion. Death overhangs the early scenes: the death of Olivia's brother, to whose memory she is dedicated, and the supposed death of Viola's brother. Olivia is jested out of her mourning, and Viola is more resilient, but passion continues to be thwarted, sometimes because those who declare it are lost in the fantasies of self-love. Olivia, wooed by Orsino, Sir Andrew, and Malvolio, responds to none of them. She also is thwarted, loving Viola in the belief that she is a man. Viola in her disguise can express her love for Orsino only obliquely. The lovers' folly generates comedy, of which Olivia's fool, Feste, makes much capital. From their first appearance together, an opposition is set up between Malvolio, the professed wise man, and Feste, the professional fool. The exposure of Malvolio is engineered by Maria and Sir Toby Belch, the upholder of the festive virtues of cakes and ale. Feste joins in, and the comedy deepens disturbingly as Malvolio remains incapable of seeing the truth. The play's most positive values are embodied in the enchanting Viola, and it is her reunion with her brother, celebrated in a moving antiphon (V.i. 218–249), that resolves the action. Now there are no obstacles to the union of Viola and Orsino, Olivia and Sebastian. For them, the shadows are dispelled, but Malvolio remains unregenerate, and Sir Toby's harshness to Sir Andrew sours our view of him. After the lovers' happiness, we are left with the wise but lonely Feste's song of the wind and the rain.

V. UNROMANTIC COMEDIES AND LATER TRAGEDIES

About 1600, Shakespeare's imagination turned in new directions. Two tragedies, *Julius Caesar* and *Hamlet*, may even have been written before *Twelfth Night*. An isolated elegy, 'The Phoenix and the Turtle', dense, plangent, and probably of irrecoverable allegorical significance, appeared in Robert Chester's *Love's Martyr* in 1601. After that, there appears to be a period of uncertainty and experimentation before the full, confident achievement of the later tragedies.

All's Well That Ends Well, first printed in 1623, is usually dated 1602–3 because of its links with *Measure for Measure*, which can more confidently be assigned to 1604. Since about 1900, these plays, along with *Troilus and Cressida*, have frequently been classed as 'problem plays.' Shakespeare based the main plot of *All's Well That Ends Well* on a story from Boccaccio's *Decameron*, which he probably read in the English translation in William Painter's *Palace of Pleasure* (1566–7). He added important characters, notably the Countess; invented the sub-plot of Parolles; and elaborated both the story and the manner of its telling. In his hands, the tale of a physician's daughter who healed a king and demanded as a reward the hand of a handsome, rich and reluctant young nobleman becomes the vehicle for a discussion of many ideas about human life, especially the extent to which human virtue is innate or acquired. The sub-plot of the cowardly Parolles illumines the ideas cast up by the main plot, and the comedy of his exposure reflects upon the disgraceful behaviour of the nobleman, Bertram. Boccaccio's story employs motifs of fairy-tale and folk legend. In some ways, Shakespeare enhances its romantic nature, adding, for example, the motif of apparent resurrection which recurs frequently in his work. But his treatment of the story is generally unromantic, producing a tension between the conventionality of some of its elements and the reality of the terms in which he presents them. The play's intellectual qualities, the unromantic nature of its despicable hero, and the fact that the heroine is obliged to behave in an unladylike manner to win him, have counted against its popularity, but it fascinates by its comic brilliance, its passages of tender and delicate emotional writing, and its deeply serious concern with the events and characters that it portrays.

Measure for Measure, too, betrays a tension between conventional plot elements and psychological verisimilitude. First printed in 1623, it is based on a two-part play, *Promos and Cassandra* (1578), by George Whetstone. In his first three acts, Shakespeare involves us intimately in his characters' moral dilemmas. Claudio's sin of fornication is hardly more than a technical offence. It seems monstrous that he is condemned by Duke Vincentio's 'outward-sainted' deputy, Angelo. Isabella's scenes of pleading with Angelo are both personally and intellectually involving, and his internal crisis as he discovers his susceptibility to sexual emotion moves us even while we deplore his duplicity. The scene (III.i) in which the Duke advises Claudio to be 'absolute for death' and Claudio expresses his fear of death is a masterly demonstration of what Keats called Shakespeare's 'negative capability' in its convincing expression of opposed attitudes.

After this point, Shakespeare changes the focus. The Duke, in his manipulations, becomes a surrogate playwright. Claudio's fate interests us, yet he appears once only and has a single, brief speech. Angelo becomes a subject of argument rather than an object of psychological exploration. In the final scene, much is left to the interpreters. Isabella and the brother she had believed dead are given no words to speak on their reunion, nor does she make any verbal response to the Duke's two, unexpected proposals of marriage. Yet the scene works up to an exciting climax as the Duke tests Isabella's capacity to exercise mercy, and, as in *All's Well That Ends Well*, a silent moment of kneeling has great theatrical power. *Measure for Measure* is passionately and explicitly concerned with moral issues. Each of the 'good' characters fails in some respect; none of the evil ones lacks some redeeming quality. Even Barnardine, the drunken, convicted murderer, is finally forgiven his 'earthly faults'. We are all, in the last analysis, 'desperately mortal.'

The problems of *Troilus and Cressida* differ from those of *All's Well That Ends Well* and *Measure for Measure*. We do not know how long it had been written before its entry in the Stationers' Register on 7 February 1603. The statement made then that it had been played at the Globe was repeated on the original title-page of the 1609 quarto, but this page was withdrawn and an added, anonymous epistle described it as 'a new play, never staled with the stage, never clapperclawed with the palms of the vulgar, and passing full of the palm comical'. In the Folio it was originally to have appeared among the tragedies, but, perhaps because of copyright difficulties, printing was delayed and it was finally placed between the histories and the tragedies.

This draws attention to problems about the play's genre. Its inspiration is partly classical, partly medieval. Shakespeare went to the first instalment of Chapman's translation of Homer, published in 1598, and to Caxton, Lydgate, and Ovid, for the material relating to the siege of Troy, but the love story, which is a late accretion, derives largely from Chaucer's *Troilus and Criseyde*, and the underlying assumptions about the Greeks and Trojans are also generally medieval. The plot is partly historical: it deals with what was regarded as the first important event in the world's history. There is some comedy, largely satirical, in Shakespeare's handling of the story. The tone is in many ways tragic, yet no character achieves tragic stature. *Troilus and Cressida* stands alone, a uniquely exploratory work. It is in every way uncompromising. The language is difficult, the action frequently slow, the dialogue philosophical. Great characters of antiquity—Agamemnon, Achilles, Ajax, Hector—are portrayed as all too fallibly human. Helen, the cause of the Trojan War, is shown on her only appearance (III.i) as a silly sensualist. The most poignant figure is Troilus. Shakespeare makes us feel the intensity of his obsession with Cressida as keenly as his bitter disillusionment at her treachery. Yet we also see him, and the other characters, from outside, as through the wrong end of a telescope, distanced, diminished. Then 'Love, friendship, charity' are seen as 'subjects all / To envious and calumniating Time' (III.iii. 173–4). Agamemnon epitomises part of the play's effect in his contrast between the 'extant moment' and 'what's past and what's to come', which is, he says, 'strewed with husks / And formless ruin of oblivion' (IV.v.166). Thersites, the professional fool, is deflating, reductive, savagely bitter, a railer rather than a jester. As he reduces war to its lowest level, so Pandarus reduces love. Pandarus's final, exhausted meditation breaks across the time-barrier of the play, linking the past with the present and suggesting a vision of all between as a 'formless ruin of oblivion.' All that is left of the great events of Troy is a dying old pander, bequeathing his diseases to the audience.

Later Tragedies

A Swiss visitor to London, Thomas Platter, saw a play about Julius Caesar on 21 September 1599. Probably this was an early performance of Shakespeare's play, in which he turns again to politics. Drawing heavily on Thomas North's fine translation of Plutarch's *Lives of the Noble Grecians and Romans* (1579), he turns history into drama, unerringly finding the right style for the subject; the language is classical in its lucidity and eloquence. And he succeeds once again in relating the particular to the general. Characteristically, the first scene sounds a basic theme: the citizens 'make holiday to see Caesar, and to rejoice in his triumph', yet the Tribunes denigrate him, and their comments on Pompey, the last popular hero, suggest both the transitoriness of human glory and the fickleness of the mob, which will be much exploited later in the play. Caesar dominates the action even after his death, yet Cassius, Brutus, and Mark Antony are of no less interest. Brutus is one of Shakespeare's more problematic characters. He is 'with himself at war' (I.ii.46), and is easily seen as an adumbration of the later tragic heroes. Self-doubt, perhaps subconscious, is suggested by the rhetoric with which he dresses up the inglorious deed in noble but hollow words: 'Let's be sacrificers, but not butchers, Caius' (II.i. 166). Soothing self-delusion contrasts with brutal reality as he talks of 'waving our red weapons o'er our heads' crying 'Peace, freedom, and liberty!' (III.i. 110–111). What this leads to is the senseless and ferocious murder of Cinna the poet (III.iii).

The Romans were especially associated with rhetoric; it is also one of the dramatist's instruments. In this play Shakespeare examines its uses and abuses. With it Cassius seduces Brutus, and Brutus deceives himself and hopes to justify his actions. Caesar creates glory for himself by a rhetoric of action as well as words; and the Forum scene (III.ii) magnificently demonstrates the power of emotive speech to sway men, to lower a crowd into a mob, to overwhelm reason by passion. At its climax we take aesthetic pleasure in the rhetorical virtuosity with which Shakespeare's artistry endows Antony as he calmly, intellectually manipulates the crowd, finally standing at the still centre of the storm of his own creation. Words continue to be important: in the quarrel of Brutus and Cassius (IV.iii), in Antony's taunt that Brutus has tried to disguise his guilt with 'good words' (V.i.30), in the fact that false words cause Cassius's death (V.iii). Antony ends the play with fine words about Brutus: but are they true? Do we know Brutus better than Antony did? Does Shakespeare end with a totally affirmative statement, or an implied question?—with an endorsement of the verdict of history, or a hint that history has its own rhetoric, no more to be trusted than any other of the words of men?

With *Hamlet*, we may feel, Shakespeare's return to tragic territory is complete, yet some critics have classed this work, written and acted by 26 July 1602 (when it was entered on

Richard Burbage, the leading player of Shakespeare's company, the Lord Chamberlain's Men, and the first to play Hamlet.   *Governors of the Dulwich College Picture Gallery, London.*

the Stationers' Register) as a problem play. Its rapid popularity is attested by the publication of a pirated, seriously corrupt text—the bad quarto—in 1603. A much better text, apparently based on Shakespeare's manuscript, appeared in the following year. This 'good' quarto has about 230 lines which are not in the theatrically influenced First Folio text (1623), which however adds about 80 lines. Editors print a composite version. Shakespeare's source may have been a play, now lost and referred to as the Ur-*Hamlet*, known to have existed by 1589.

Hamlet is exceptionally long and ambitious. It is far-ranging in linguistic effect. Shakespeare's virtuosity enables him to create distinctive styles with which to individualize characters such as Claudius, Polonius, the Gravediggers, and Osric. The play offers a wide variety of theatrical entertainment, including such well-tried pleasures as a ghost, a play-within-the-play, a mad scene, a duel, and several deaths. Emotionally, too, the range is wide. This is Shakespeare's most humorous tragedy. Yet the comedy is never incidental. Polonius's verbal deviousness and Osric's affected circumlocutions, comic in themselves, are among the many barriers to honest communication which intensify Hamlet's tragic dilemma. The gravediggers' phlegmatic humour is an essential element in Hamlet's contemplation of death. And Hamlet's own wit has both a princely elegance which adds to the sense of waste evoked by his destruction, and a savage intellectuality which defines his isolation from those around him and serves him as a weapon against hypocrisy and deception.

Hamlet's appeal derives from his youth, intelligence, charm, vulnerability, and, above all, his intellectual and emotional honesty. He is a raw nerve in the Danish court, disconcertingly liable to make the instinctive rather than the conditioned response. Though this cuts him off from those around him, it puts him into a position of peculiar intimacy with the audience. And in his soliloquies, Shakespeare shows us Hamlet's own raw nerves. Hamlet lacks a distinctive style, at least until the play's closing stages. This is a symptom of his inability to identify himself, to voice his emotions from within a defined personality. But it enables him to speak in a wonderful range of styles, reflecting the openness to experience which is an essential feature of his honesty. The language of his soliloquies presents us not with conclusions, but with the very processes of his mind. Never before had dramatic language so vividly revealed 'the quick forge and working-house of thought' (*Henry V*, V Chorus. 23).

Hamlet's progress through the play is a dual exploration of outer and inner worlds. The ghost's command requires that he discover the truth about those who surround him; it leads also to intense self-questioning about his own attitudes to life and, especially, death. During this process he both undergoes and inflicts torments. He causes mental suffering to his mother and to Ophelia, for whose death he is indirectly responsible. He kills Polonius and engineers the deaths of Rosencrantz and Guildenstern. He arrives finally at the truth about the world around him. Whether he ultimately reaches a state of self-knowledge and acceptance is less certain. The new quietude which he demonstrates after his return from England suggests to some critics a fatalistic submission to worldly values; for others, it indicates rather a state of spiritual grace reflecting a full integration of his own personality along with an acknowledgement of human responsibility. Generations of readers and spectators share in Hamlet's self-questionings; it is partly because of his openness to disparate interpretation that he continues to fascinate.

Othello, given at Court on 1 November 1604, and first published in 1622, must have been written in 1602 or 1603. Like *Romeo and Juliet*, it is based, not on history or legend, but on a contemporary fiction. Shakespeare here transforms a rather sordid tale from Giraldo Cinthio's *Hecatommithi* (1565), which he seems to have read in Italian. Whereas *Hamlet* is discursive and amplificatory, *Othello* is swift, concise, and tautly constructed. Most of Shakespeare's tragic heroes are royal figures whose fate is inextricably bound up with their nations, and whose suffering has a metaphysical dimension. Othello is a servant of the state, not a ruler. His play is in some senses a domestic tragedy, in which we are invited to concentrate on individual human beings rather than to see a connexion between their fates and universal, elemental forces. All Shakespeare's tragedies show evil at work. Only in *Othello* is it concentrated in one, centrally placed intriguer. Iago is the playwright within the play. He controls the plot, makes it up as he goes along with improvisatory genius; and, also like the playwright, he retreats ultimately into silence. He is several times called a devil, and historians have seen him as a development of the stereotype of the Vice, an allegorical presentation of an abstract concept. On stage, he is as much of a human being as any of the other characters.

In some of Shakespeare's plays, we are frequently invited to see the stage action as emblematic of a larger dramatic conflict being played out on a universal stage. The significance of *Othello* resides more purely in the passions and fates of the human beings whom we see before us. But Shakespeare does not present the tale as a documentary imitation of reality. We are made conscious of paradox. Iago, who reveals his villainy to the audience, is 'honest' to everyone in the play except Roderigo. Othello's physical blackness joins with the traditional symbolism of black and white as a fruitful source of irony and ambiguity. The language draws our attention to general concepts, and causes us to reflect on the varieties of human behaviour. Iago is a rationalist. His characteristic language is a cynically reductive prose; he speaks of the act of love as a bestial coupling: 'An old black ram/Is tupping your white ewe' (I.i. 89–90). Othello is a nobly credulous idealist. His 'free and open nature' makes him think 'men honest that but seem to be so' (I.iii. 393–4). His susceptibility to Iago's corruptive power is a concomitant of his virtue. For him, Shakespeare created a magniloquent verse-style suggestive rather of imagination than of intellectuality. The contrast between these two, the way that Iago drags Othello down to his own level, and that Othello, too late, shakes himself clear of him, forms the central dramatic action. The universality of the play lies in our consciousness of Iago's plausibility and our sympathy with Othello's insecurities. Inside the most loving human relationship lie seeds which, once germinated, may destroy it. In Claudius's words:

> There lies within the very flame of love
> A kind of wick or snuff that will abate it.
> (*Hamlet*, IV.vii. 114–115)

In *King Lear*, Shakespeare compounded a story from legendary history with one from prose fiction. Holinshed tells briefly the tale of King Lear. Other versions (all ending happily) include a play, *King Leir*, written by 1594, which is one of Shakespeare's sources. Its publication in 1605 may have given him the impetus to write his play, first recorded in a Court performance on 26 December 1606 and printed in 1608. His subplot of the Earl of Gloucester derives from Sir Philip Sidney's *Arcadia* (pub. 1590). His interweaving of the two stories is crucial to his design. Lear and Gloucester are both faulty, but not wicked. Lear has two evil daughters and a good one, Gloucester has an evil son and a good one. Each misjudges his offspring, favours but is turned against by the evil ones, wrongs the good one, suffers as a consequence, learns the truth, and dies. Gloucester's error and suffering are mainly physical. His evil son, Edmund, is a bastard, begotten in adultery. The climax of Gloucester's suffering comes when Lear's daughters, Goneril and Regan, put out his eyes. Lear's fault lies in his warped judgement, and his suffering is primarily mental; its climax is his madness after his daughters have cast him out into the storm. Other characters relate to this patterning. The Fool, physically frail, 'labours to out-jest' Lear's 'heart-struck injuries' (III.i. 16–17) and to bring him to an understanding of his situation by way of his mind, in snatches of song, witticisms, paradoxes, and parables. Kent, the other servant who remains faithful to Lear through the storm, is more practical, ministering rather to his physical needs. Edmund's sexuality, which in his adulterous relationship with both Goneril and Regan brings about his downfall, recalls his father's. Edgar, Gloucester's virtuous son, metamorphosed into Poor Tom, is of both physical and mental help to his father. The callous, sceptical rationality of Edmund, Goneril, and Regan is opposed to the imagination and sympathy of Edgar, the Fool, and Cordelia.

The employment of the two basic components of human life, the body and the mind, as a structural principle reflects the depth of Shakespeare's concern with fundamentals in this play. In his examination of the values by which men live, he stresses the pre-Christian setting of his story, avoiding all suggestions of religious dogma. His play explores the paradoxes of value. Those who are committed to the world and the flesh destroy themselves. They are deceived by false appearances; so, initially, are Gloucester and Lear. But these two come to 'see better' (I.i. 157) when they trust the mind rather than the body. Nowhere is this more apparent than in Shakespeare's causing Gloucester's apprehension of the truth about his sons to follow immediately upon his blinding: 'A man may see how this world goes with no eyes' (IV.vi. 150–1). Lear and Gloucester go through purgatory, and commune with one another in the amazing scene on Dover cliff. Lear's cynical and disillusioned statements here are only one facet of the play. After this comes his return to sanity and his reconciliation with Cordelia, which is also a reconciliation with life. Nor is this negated by Cordelia's death. This relentlessly unsentimental play puts Lear through the greatest mental torment, but ultimately the man who had vowed never again to see Cordelia's face seeks desperately in her eyes for signs of life. He has learned that she is indeed 'most rich, being poor;/Most choice, forsaken; and most lov'd, despis'd' (I.i. 250–251). His final outpouring of love is unselfish; she can do nothing for him now. Her body is dead and useless, but the values for which she stood are those that endure.

Macbeth, written probably in 1606, is easily Shakespeare's shortest tragedy. Its topic was particularly relevant to the patron of his company, James I, and the only surviving text, of 1623, may have been specially written or adapted for Court performance. Holinshed again provided the basic narrative, but, as in *King Lear*, Shakespeare treated it with much more freedom than in the English histories. To a greater extent even than in *King Lear*, he seems more interested in general ideas than in historical accuracy or particularity of characterization. Many of the characters are purely functional. Duncan is primarily a symbol of the values that Macbeth is to overthrow. He is counterbalanced by the equally generalized Weird Sisters. Even Banquo figures mainly as a measure of the norm from which Macbeth deviates. The witches, with their incantations, spells, and grotesque rituals, suggest evil as a universal force which can be tapped and channelled through human agents.

Like her counterparts in *King Lear*, Lady Macbeth, the play's principal human embodiment of evil, attempts to deny the powers of the imagination. A speech from *All's Well That Ends Well* epitomizes this aspect of *Macbeth*. 'They say miracles are past', says Lafeu, 'and we have our philosophical persons to make modern and familiar things supernatural and causeless. Hence is it that we make trifles of terrors, ensconcing ourselves into seeming knowledge when we should submit ourselves to an unknown fear' (II.iii. 1–6). Lady Macbeth seeks to reduce 'supernatural and causeless'— inexplicable—things to the level of the 'modern'—commonplace—'and familiar': 'The sleeping and the dead/Are but as pictures'. . . . 'A little water clears us of this deed' (II.ii. 53–4, 67). This is the 'seeming knowledge' which turns 'terrors' into 'trifles', and refuses to acknowledge the 'unknown fear' of which Macbeth is so vividly conscious. His imaginative visions almost overwhelm his reason. Better for him if they had, for the play acts out the truth of Lafeu's statement. Lady Macbeth's rationalistic urgings of her husband are at odds with her own incantation 'Come you spirits. . . .' (I.v. 37ff), and when her reason breaks down, her self-assurance is seen to be only a 'seeming knowledge' which gives way, too late, to the 'unknown fear'. Her sleep-walking scene, a soliloquy unheard even by its speaker, is a technically brilliant device to reveal the subconscious acknowledgement in her divided being of 'things supernatural and causeless'.

In his last three tragedies, Shakespeare returns to more fully documented periods of history, and, in two of them, to a more particularized presentation of it. The exception is *Timon of Athens*, a problematic play. Thematic resemblances to *King Lear* and *Coriolanus* along with stylistic evidence cause it generally to be dated 1606–8, but the state of the text, first printed in 1623, is such that study of it can be only provisional. As it appears to have been printed from an uncompleted manuscript, it is exceptionally interesting to the student of Shakespeare's working methods. There are signs of the rapidity of composition with which he was credited by his contemporaries. He seems to have been anxious to lay down the groundwork, to evolve a shape and structure which could later have been filled in. He concentrates on the central role, which is long and taxing. Minor characters might have been developed later; there is uncertainty about some of their names, and there are many anomalies in the action. While some of the language, both verse and prose, is polished, other passages are obviously in draft, veering between verse and prose. There are strong lines of recurrent imagery which might later have been more subtly worked into the structure. The acts of eating and drinking, for instance, and the opposition between roots and gold, take on heavily symbolic associations. As in *King Lear*, Shakespeare is concerned with the difference between 'true need', which can be satisfied by roots, and superfluity, represented by banquets and gold.

We usually read the play in an edited version, in which some of the imperfections have been smoothed away. Much more tinkering is needed to create a performable text. The result is that this play is peculiarly open to interpretation, raising more questions than it answers. Its strongly schematic quality allies it more closely with *King Lear* and *Macbeth* than with *Coriolanus* and *Antony and Cleopatra*. It is based on Plutarch, and treats Timon's story as a two-part structure: Timon in prosperity, followed by Timon in adversity. In the first part, the rich, lavish, magnanimous lord is contrasted with Apemantus, the cynic philosopher. As Timon learns that he has spent all he owned, his flatterers are revealed, in skilfully satirical episodes, as a 'knot of mouth-friends' (III.vi. 89), and Apemantus is partly justified. An awkwardly unrelated scene, which might well have become the climax of a sub-plot, shows the Athenians' ingratitude to Alcibiades. The second part, as it stands, is virtually an interrupted soliloquy by Timon, in which he encounters those he had known in his former way of life. In his misanthropy induced by disillusionment he is as extravagant as he had previously been in his generosity. Now he resembles Apemantus, as a fine scene (IV.iii) between them shows, but Apemantus is a contented cynic, whereas Timon needs to give full emotional vent to his rejection of mankind. The appearance of his steward, Flavius, comes as a reminder of the possibility of love, loyalty, and friendship, and Timon himself accepts, though with difficulty, that he is mistaken in his wholesale denunciation of mankind. The final scenes, showing Timon's death and Alcibiades's successful campaign against Athens, are sketchy.

Timon of Athens is underdeveloped and inconclusive. Its tone is harsh and bitter, though other attitudes are present in Flavius and other servants, in Alcibiades, even in Timon's tirades, which suggest a desire to be reconciled with humanity by the very force with which he rejects it. The play has pungent invective, clever satire, a few passages of noble poetry, a clear if crude structure, and some profound revelations of humanity. We can only guess what it might have become if Shakespeare had completed it.

His remaining tragedies, *Coriolanus* and *Antony and Cleopatra*, both first published in 1623, are based closely on Plutarch, and reflect Plutarch's concern with the idiosyncrasies and oddities of human character, and with the way such characteristics shape national as well as human destinies. *Coriolanus* (probably written 1607–8) tells a story of war and peace, love and hate. The broad framework is one of national warfare, epitomized in a personal conflict between Caius Marcius, later Coriolanus, and the Volscian leader, Tullus Aufidius. Their relationship is ambiguous; after Coriolanus has been banished from Rome, Aufidius welcomes him with 'I . . . do contest/As hotly and as nobly with thy love/As ever in ambitious strength I did/Contend against thy valour' (IV.v. 109–113). Strife within Rome also resolves itself into a largely personal conflict, between Coriolanus and the two unscrupulous Tribunes. His arrogance, inseparable from his valour, brings about his banishment, so that from being the enemy within the state he becomes identified with the enemy outside it. He is at conflict, too, within his own family. His mother, Volumnia, eager for his fame, expresses her love for him in terms that might rather betoken hatred: 'O, he is wounded, I thank the gods for't' (II.i. 114). Sharing his hatred of the commons, she yet advises him to dissemble with his nature to catch their votes, and so forces a conflict within Coriolanus himself. His efforts to play the part for which she casts him produce some comedy, but the issues of integrity and honour with which the play is concerned are focussed in his ultimate refusal to do so, 'Lest I surcease to honour mine own truth,/And by my body's action teach my mind/A most inherent baseness.' (III.ii. 121–2). In his consequent banishment he has to pretend hatred of those he loves. When his family come to plead with him, he is forced into self-recognition: 'I melt, and am not/Of stronger earth than others.' (V.iii. 28–9). His mother insists again on the need for compromise, for, if he conquers Rome, he conquers her. He 'holds her by the hand, silent' in a moment of sub-mission which is also a moment of self-examination.

> O mother, mother!
> What have you done? Behold, the heavens do ope,
> The gods look down, and this unnatural scene
> They laugh at. O my mother, mother! O!
> You have won a happy victory to Rome;
> But for your son—believe it, O believe it!—
> Most dangerously you have with him prevail'd,
> If not most mortal to him. But let it come.
>
> (V.iv. 182–9)

Acknowledging that he can no longer maintain a god-like aloofness from natural emotion, he accepts the full burden of his humanity, and also the inevitability of his death. 'But let it come' is the equivalent in this play to Hamlet's 'The readiness is all', and to 'Ripeness is all' in *King Lear*. But it is the final paradox of the mother-son relationship in *Coriolanus* that Volumnia, in calling forth a full expression of her son's love, brings about his death. Thus closely are love and hate allied.

Coriolanus is a great achievement of the intellect and the historical imagination. Its characteristic style seems to be carved out of granite. *Antony and Cleopatra*, written about the same time (it was entered in the Stationers' Register on 20 May 1608), is less intellectual and even more imaginative. Few of Shakespeare's plays derive their greatness less from their design, more from their characterization and language. Its style is supple, relaxed, and sensuous. Cleopatra rivals Falstaff as Shakespeare's greatest feat of characterization, and her 'infinite variety' is created largely by the flexibility and range of the language with which Shakespeare endows her. The scope of *Antony and Cleopatra* is vast. The action takes place over an area which seems particularly large because characters move so easily from one part of it to another, far distant. Empires are at stake; the play is peopled by their leaders. Nevertheless, much of the play's setting is domestic. Many scenes portray the home life of Egypt's queen, and Shakespeare's greatness as a dramatic writer shows itself particularly in a dialogue of nuance which gives great significance to oblique statements, exclamations, pauses, and silences. So when Cleopatra is brought to comfort Antony after his 'doting' withdrawal from battle:

Eros	Nay, gentle madam, to him! Comfort him.
Iras	Do, most dear Queen.
Charmian	Do? Why, what else?
Cleopatra	Let me sit down. O Juno!
Antony	No, no, no, no, no.
Eros	See you here, sir?
Antony	O, fie, fie, fie!
Charmian	Madam!
Iras	Madam, O good Empress!
Eros	Sir, sir!

(III.ix. 25–34)

Or, in one of Shakespeare's most pregnant monosyllables:

Thyreus	He [Caesar] knows that you embrace not Antony As you did love, but as you fear'd him.
Cleopatra	O!

(III.xiii. 56–7)

But when necessary Shakespeare writes to the very height of his eloquence. Language is intimately related to form, and so a double-tragedy presents special problems. In Shakespeare's only other one, *Romeo and Juliet*, the hero and heroine at least die in the same scene; here, their deaths are necessarily separated, and Shakespeare averts anti-climax in the second, Cleopatra's, partly by introducing a new character—the Clown who carries the instrument of her death—partly by the richly symbolic nature of her conversation with him, and, above all, by the transcendent poetry of her closing speeches.

The tension between Egyptian and Roman values in *Antony and Cleopatra* is an aspect of Shakespeare's recurrent portrayal of the opposing claims of festivity and austerity, licence and discipline, in plays such as *Twelfth Night* and *1* and *2 Henry IV*. Style and imagery cause us to relate this conflict to the divergent claims of the imagination and the reason, and to man's sense of the potential glory of human achievement along with his awareness of the limitations imposed by mortality. So, as in *Julius Caesar* and *Troilus and Cressida*, we can both live in the moment and see it in relation to eternity. Antony is 'the triple pillar of the world' and 'a 'strumpet's fool' (I.i. 12–13); 'Kingdoms are clay' (I.i. 35), 'Royal Egypt' is 'No more but e'en a woman. . . .' (IV.xv. 71–3), and the instrument of Cleopatra's death is a worm. These extremes are shown not simply in opposition, but sometimes in double perspective, at other times, movingly, in dissolution from one to the other: Antony, dying, 'cannot hold this visible shape' (IV.xiv. 14), 'The crown o' th' earth doth melt' (IV.xv. 63). Ultimately Shakespeare seems to support the values of sensitivity and the imagination. In Falstaff he had done so covertly; here, he does so openly. Enobarbus learns the limitations of reason, and regrets that he has followed its dictates; and Cleopatra's ultimate celebration of the flesh in the spirit creates a vision which may lack substance, but is glorious while it lasts. No other tragic character except, perhaps, Wagner's Isolde, dies with such exaltation.

VI. LATE SHAKESPEARE

We saw that Shakespeare's return to tragedy overlapped with his later experiments in comedy. Similarly, while he was writing his last tragedies his thoughts seem to have been turning again to comedy, though only, as we should expect, because he saw new possibilities in the form. Four of his late plays make up perhaps the most closely interrelated group among his output. All employ motifs of romance literature. Their plots include highly improbable and supernatural elements. They tell of high-born families and lovers separated by catastrophe, sometimes natural, sometimes humanly contrived. They span large areas of space and time, and involve leading characters in great suffering. Settings are remote. The presentation of character tends to the general and the ideal. Suffering is overcome, obstacles to reunion and reconciliation are removed, sometimes as a result of supernatural intervention, and harmony is restored.

All these characteristics can be found in Shakespeare's earlier comedies, but they are present in greater concentration in what are variously known as the Last Plays, the Romances, or the Late Romances. And these plays have more than superficial resemblances. Shakespeare was never one-track minded. Even plays which employ a relatively narrow focus, such as *Richard II* and *King Lear*, have a range of emotional impact. *Timon of Athens* shows the extremes of a man's experience but, as Apemantus says, little between them: 'The middle of humanity thou never knewest, but the extremity of both ends' (IV.iii. 299–301). In his late plays, Shakespeare shows a wish to encompass the extremes in a yoking of opposites which will confine a full range of human experience within the local and temporal limitations of a play, and will synthesize the disparate elements so as to allow each to exert its energy.

External influences have sometimes been adduced as an explanation of Shakespeare's change of direction. The increased use of spectacle in the late plays has been attributed both to the growing popularity of masques at Court and to the acquisition by the King's Men of an indoor theatre, the Blackfriars, which would offer increased opportunities for spectacular staging. Yet the company continued to use the Globe, and the late plays were performed there as well. The first, *Pericles*, presents almost as many problems as *Timon of Athens*. It may have been written before both the purchase of the Blackfriars and the composition of the last of the tragedies. It is based on the old story of Apollonius of Tyre, told by John Gower in his *Confessio Amantis* (1385–93), and on the version of it in Laurence Twine's *The Pattern of Painful Adventures* (?1576). Shakespeare had already used the tale, in *The Comedy of Errors*, and his attention may have been drawn to it again by the reissue of Twine's book in 1607. Like *Antony and Cleopatra*, *Pericles* was entered in the Stationers' Register on 20 May 1608 by Edward Blount, who, however, published neither. A prose romance by George Wilkins, *The Painful Adventures of Pericles, Prince of Tyre*, published in 1608, refers to the play on the title-page and borrows from both it and Twine. *Pericles* was very popular on the stage, but the text published in 1609 is corrupt. It was reprinted five times by 1635, but Heminges and Condell omitted it from the First Folio, presumably because they knew how defective this text was, and could not find a better. It is so badly garbled, especially in the first two acts, as to have raised doubts about its title-page ascription to Shakespeare, and some scholars believe that it was either his revision of another dramatist's work, or a collaboration.

Editors of *Pericles*, as of *Timon of Athens*, smooth away some of its defects. If we read it with sympathy, we can imagine that the authentic play stood high among Shakespeare's achievements. The device of a presenter, the poet Gower, is used to frame and control the far-flung narrative, and the archaic style and naive tone of his choruses induce the proper mood for the reception of a tale of wonder. The initial stages of the action, in which Pericles gains a wife, Thaisa, are episodic, but it gains in concentration with the birth at sea of their daughter, Marina, and Thaisa's apparent death. Even in its damaged state, some of the verse associated with these events has a unique magic. Marina is a mystically ideal portrayal of the power of chastity, and her presence in a brothel whose inmates are sketched with truly Shakespearian immediacy is one illustration of the play's use of extremes. As in all the romances, there is a strong sense that life is controlled by inscrutable, if ultimately beneficent, powers, symbolized by sea and storm. Thus, Marina laments:

> Ay me! poor maid,
> Born in a tempest, when my mother died,
> This world to me is like a lasting storm,
> Whirring me from my friends.
>
> (IV.i. 18–21)

Out of the tempest comes a calm of which music is the apt symbol. Thaisa, believed dead and committed to the waves, is revived to the sound of instruments, and Marina sings to her father to try to restore him from the coma into which

grief has driven him. Their protracted reunion scene, masterly in its control, draws from Pericles lines in which he
expresses two recurrent ideas of these plays: the close relationship between the apparent extremes of pain and joy, and
the capacity of the young to renew their parents' lives:

> O Helicanus, strike me, honour'd sir;
> Give me a gash, put me to present pain,
> Lest this great sea of joys rushing upon me
> O'erbear the shores of my mortality,
> And drown me with their sweetness. O, come hither,
> Thou that beget'st him that did thee beget;
> Thou that wast born at sea, buried at Tharsus,
> And found at sea again!
>
> (V.i. 189–196)

When Marina's identity is established, the music of the
spheres induces in Pericles a vision of Diana leading to the
revelation that Thaisa is alive and to the miraculously joyful
outcome of the action.

Shakespeare appears to have followed *Pericles* with *Cymbe-
line*, composed probably 1609–10 and first published in 1623,
in which he implausibly yokes together Roman Britain and
Renaissance Italy. The historical background is freely based
on Holinshed and the intrigue tale derives from Boccaccio.
The play is peopled by antithetical characters: some, such as
Imogen, Pisanio, Belarius, and those children of nature,
Arviragus and Guiderius, are paragons of virtue; others, such
as Cloten and the Queen, are 'Too bad for bad report' (I.i. 17).
Iachimo moves from outright villainy to penitence; Posthumus from virtue to debasement brought about by Iachimo's
deception, and back to virtue again. Some of the characters
seem the reverse of their true selves: the Queen conceals her
villainy from most of those around her, Posthumus is made
to believe that Imogen is false to him; some—Imogen,
Cloten, Posthumus—are disguised for part of the action;
others—Arviragus and Guiderius—are unaware of their own
true identity. The plot is based on both national and personal
opposition: Britain and Rome are at war; many of the
characters are at enmity with one another. The design of
some of the scenes stresses the falsity of appearance, as when
Cloten's attendant lords comment upon him in ironical

asides (I.ii), or the Queen's villainous plotting is framed by her instructions to her ladies about gathering flowers (I.v). The language, too, is frequently antithetical. The play's oppositions reach their climax in the scene (IV.ii) in which Imogen, disguised as a boy and believed to be dead as the result of the Queen's drugs, is mourned by the two young men, who, unknown to any of them, are her brothers, and lain to rest beside the headless body of Cloten. She has said she values him less than the 'meanest garment' of her husband, Posthumus; now he is dressed in Posthumus's clothes. The beauty of the verse in which Imogen is mourned and of the flowers with which the bodies are strewn is juxtaposed with the hideous spectacle of the headless corpse; and her waking speech, in which she identifies Cloten with Posthumus, is perhaps the most bizarre and daring in the whole of Shakespeare.

If this scene gives us both heaven and hell simultaneously, the final one gives us heaven alone. It is prepared for by the appearance of Jupiter to the sleeping Posthumus, which raises the action on to a plane of the ideal. The multiple dénouements of the final scene, in which all disguises are removed, all identities made known, and all misunderstandings removed, strike with the wonder—and, unless tactfully performed, the implausibility—of the miraculous achievement of the impossible. In the play's closing lines, Cymbeline celebrates the resolution of discord into harmony:

> . . . . . let
> A Roman and a British ensign wave
> Friendly together . . . . . .
> . . . . . Never was a war did cease,
> Ere bloody hands were wash'd, with such a peace.

Cymbeline is a fantasy, an exercise in virtuosity, intricate in style and self-conscious in its artifice. In *The Winter's Tale*, which Simon Forman saw at the Globe on 15 May 1611 and which was probably written later than *Cymbeline*, Shakespeare engages more closely with reality. The story, based on a prose romance of the 1580's, Robert Greene's *Pandosto*, covers sixteen years, and moves in space from the Sicilian court to the Bohemian countryside, and back to the court again. The central character, Leontes, King of Sicily, passes through extremes of emotion, from the near tragedy of his suffering, culminating in the death of his son and the apparent deaths of his wife and daughter, through the 'saint-like sorrow' (V.i. 2) of his penitence to the rapture of the ending, in which he is reunited with those he had believed dead.

Shakespeare fully exploits the variety of theatrical entertainment inherent in this material. But whereas *Cymbeline* works largely through the juxtaposition of opposed elements, *The Winter's Tale* is notable rather for the transitions by which the movement between extremes is controlled. Leontes's obsessive sexual jealousy is vividly experienced, but the audience is partly distanced from it by Paulina's ironical attitude and by the grotesqueness of Leontes's language. The first movement of the play reaches a powerful climax in the trial of his Queen, Hermione (III.ii). Shakespeare skilfully guides us into the idealized pastoralism of the middle section by presenting the terrible (and improbable) subsequent events—the abandonment of Leontes's infant daughter, Perdita, on the shore of Bohemia along with the deaths of Antigonus and the entire crew of the ship on which they travelled—through the eyes of the comically uninvolved Clown and with the assistance of the notorious Bear (III.iii).

Long gaps of time are inconvenient to dramatists. Shakespeare solves the problem in *The Winter's Tale* by giving Time a prominent place in the play's structure of ideas. The opening scene includes a poetic evocation of childhood illusions of timelessness (I.i. 62–74); Time makes a personal appearance, as the Chorus (IV.i); Florizel's love speech magically suggests that Perdita's beauty, and his love for her, can suspend the passage of time (IV.iv. 134–143); the concluding episodes show time offering opportunities for repentance and redemption; and a sense of renewal is created by the fact that the son and daughter of the estranged kings bring about their parents' reconciliation by their marriage. Also prominent among the play's ideas is the antithesis, commonplace in the thought of the period, between art and nature. Their relationship is explicitly discussed in IV.iv, and a kind of art is apparent in the exercise of the will by which Leontes expresses his penitence and the lovers control their ardour.

These ideas merge in the final scene. Shakespeare departs from his source in keeping Hermione alive, and the daring stroke of making her pose as her own statue is symbolically appropriate as well as theatrically effective. Hermione's resurrection is a conquest over time. Self-control brings its rewards as art melts into nature and the stone becomes flesh. The play ends in the joy and wonder characteristic of romance, but they are counterpointed by our consciousness of the suffering out of which the miracle has emerged.

Shakespeare's last independently written play, *The Tempest*, published in 1623, was performed at Court on 1 November 1611; probably he wrote it during that year. In its composition he drew on his reading of Ovid, Montaigne, and contemporary travel literature, but he wove the plot out of his own imagination, creating a fantasy which is his most overtly symbolical drama. We have no reason to believe that he knew he was coming to the end of his career, but it is easy to see this as an exceptionally personal play. In it, he disciplines the sprawling material of romance by confining it within the limits of the neo-classical unities which he had employed only once before, in the early *Comedy of Errors*. Instead of following the events of the tale from beginning to end and place to place, he concentrates the action into a few hours and the locale into a few acres. We see only the end of the story; the earlier stages are recapitulated in Prospero's narration. This creates a tension between form and content which finds many correspondences in the action. Like Oberon, Duke Vincentio, and Iago before him, Prospero is a playwright within the play. He seeks to discipline his erring fellows, and needs self-discipline to do so. His power, though magical, is limited. He can create visions, but they are easily destroyed: the masque vanishes into air at his recollection of Caliban's malice. Prospero can exercise moral influence, but only over those who are predisposed to receive it. Alonso and Ferdinand are better for their experiences, but Antonio and Sebastian remain unregenerate.

It is easy to see this as an allegory of the artist and his work. The masque can only fulfil its purpose of pleasing and instructing if it is received with sympathy. The artist needs a fit audience. *The Tempest* itself may be regarded as one of the glories of mankind or a load of waste paper. To this extent it may properly be considered as an autobiographical document. But it is very much more. The compression of the plot necessitates a high degree of stylization. The resultant symbolic action and generalized characterization open the play to a wide range of interpretation. Though Prospero can be seen as an artist, he can be seen also as a father, a teacher, a scholar, a scientist, a magistrate, an explorer, a ruler, even a god. We can discuss the play in terms of the artist and his public, but it relates also to many of the concepts that we have found recurring in Shakespeare's work: art and nature; nature and fortune; imagination and the reason; justice and mercy; sin and retribution; guilt and repentance; right rule and rebellion; illusion and reality; self-deception and self-knowledge.

The Tempest resists clear-cut allegorical readings; this is a measure of its success. It is a supremely poetic drama, not just because it includes some of Shakespeare's greatest poetry, but because it speaks, as the greatest poetry does, on many levels, universally relevant and—if we can hear Ariel's music—universally effective.

Shakespeare and Fletcher

Shakespeare's successor as leading dramatist for the King's Men was John Fletcher (1579–1625), known for his collaboration with Francis Beaumont (c. 1584–1616), who gave up writing for the stage about 1613. At about this time, Fletcher appears to have begun to collaborate with Shakespeare. *Henry VIII*, published as the last of the Histories in the First Folio (1623), was in performance, possibly for the first time, at the Globe when the theatre burned down on 29 June 1613. For a long time its attribution to Shakespeare was unquestioned, but in 1850 James Spedding propounded the theory that parts of it are by Fletcher, and many other scholars have followed him in this belief. Certainly in its overall layout it is unlike the history plays that Shakespeare had written during the 1590s, though in its elegiac tone, its generalized characterization, and the sense that it conveys of destiny working itself out through human life, it has something in common with his romances. It has less variety than most of Shakespeare's plays, and presents a series of tableaux showing, as the Prologue says, 'How . . . mightiness meets misery.' We see the falls successively of Buckingham, Wolsey, and Queen Katherine, each of them eloquent in resignation. But the play works towards the birth of Anne Boleyn's child, and the last scene fulsomely celebrates not only the future Queen Elizabeth I, but also her successor, the patron of the King's Men.

> So shall she leave her blessedness to one—
> When heaven shall call her from this cloud of darkness—
> Who from the sacred ashes of her honour
> Shall star-like rise, as great in fame as she was,
> And so stand fix'd.

(V.v. 43–7)

This speech is not generally attributed to Shakespeare.

Henry VIII has been successful in the theatre. It offers several strong acting roles, and great opportunities for spectacle, which have caused it to be performed particularly at times of national rejoicing, such as coronations. Some of its most effective passages, including Wolsey's well-known 'Farewell, a long farewell, to all my greatness!' (III.ii. 351) are attributed to Fletcher. According to a Stationers' Register entry of 9 September 1653, Shakespeare and Fletcher collaborated on a play called *Cardenio*, now lost, which was given twice at Court by the King's Men in the season 1613–14. A manuscript of it may have lain beyond a play called *The Double Falsehood* by Lewis Theobald, one of Shakespeare's editors, which was acted at Drury Lane in 1727 and printed the following year. The last surviving play in which Shakespeare is believed to have had a hand is *The Two Noble Kinsmen*, a tragi-comedy written at some time between February 1613 (the date of the performance of a masque by Francis Beaumont from which it borrows a dance) and 31 October 1614 (when Jonson's *Bartholomew Fair*, which contains an allusion to it, was first performed). It was omitted from the First Folio, but appeared in 1634 as 'written by the memorable worthies of their time, Mr John Fletcher, and Mr William Shakespeare, Gent.' The passages generally attributed to Shakespeare make up about one-third of the play, and are characteristic of his late verse style.

The works surveyed in the preceding pages have given Shakespeare his status as the greatest writer in English, perhaps in any language. Like most great artists, he built on foundations laid by other men. His genius was not primarily innovative, though, as we have seen, he constantly experimented with dramatic forms and techniques. The theatrical medium appears to have provided a necessary challenge which sometimes constrained him. In plays such as *The Comedy of Errors*, *As You Like It*, *Othello*, and *The Tempest* we feel an absolute matching of content and form. In others, such as *The Merchant of Venice*, *Hamlet*, *King Lear*, and *Cymbeline*, signs of struggle may be discerned. The teeming fullness of Shakespeare's creativity results sometimes in writing of convoluted, even bizarre density and in structures which make exceptional demands in both complexity and length on theatre audiences.

Yet his powers as an entertainer were such that his plays can appeal on many levels. The best of them are dramatic and linguistic structures of infinite complexity which explore mankind's most fundamental concerns. Even in so brief a study as this we have seen something of his interest in government of both the individual and the state, in the moral pressures of society upon the individual, in the part played by reason and the imagination in human affairs, in the need for self-knowledge, in the relation between the past and the present, and in the power of language. These are philosophical questions. Shakespeare uses the emblematic and metaphorical techniques of the poetic dramatist to body them forth with a wholly human particularity which is as recognizable today as it was to his first audiences.

VII. THE PUBLICATION OF SHAKESPEARE'S WORKS

Shakespeare seems to have concerned himself with the printing of only two of his works, the poems *Venus and Adonis* (1593) and *The Rape of Lucrece* (1594). These volumes bear his only dedications, both to the Earl of Southampton, and are carefully printed. As for the plays, Shakespeare apparently regarded performance as publication. The scripts belonged to the company, which in general was not anxious to release them for performance. But there was a market for printed plays, and several of Shakespeare's appeared first in corrupt texts which seem to have been assembled from memory by some of the actors who appeared in them. These are known as the 'bad' quartos. Sometimes, however, printers were able to work from Shakespeare's own manuscripts, or transcripts of them. Texts produced from such authoritative sources are known, even when they are poorly printed, as 'good' quartos. Altogether, nineteen of Shakespeare's plays appeared in separately printed editions in Shakespeare's lifetime, and *Othello* followed in 1622. Some appeared only in bad texts, some only in good ones, and some in both. The Sonnets were printed in 1609 in a good text.

After Shakespeare died, his colleagues, John Heminges and Henry Condell, undertook a collected edition of his plays. They had at their disposal the printed quartos and a number of manuscripts, some of which had been annotated for theatrical use. They brought them together in the First Folio, which appeared in 1623, with the Droeshout engraving of Shakespeare, their dedication to the brother Earls of Pembroke and Montgomery, their epistle 'To the Great Variety of Readers', several commendatory poems including the well-known one by Ben Jonson, and a list of the 'Principal Actors' in the plays. The Folio included eighteen plays not previously printed, but omitted *Pericles* and *The Two Noble Kinsmen*.

No literary manuscript by Shakespeare survives, unless we accept the attribution to him of three pages of a collaborative play, *Sir Thomas More*, of uncertain date. Otherwise the early printed editions give us our only evidence of what Shakespeare wrote. Unfortunately, this evidence is often unreliable and conflicting. There are many misprints both in the quartos and in the Folio, some obvious, some only suspected. When a play survives in both quarto and Folio there are often divergences which may be attributed to a variety of causes, including errors of transcription; printing errors; theatrical alterations, omissions, and additions; censorship; authorial revision; and so on. Even the Folio-only plays sometimes show signs of departing from the author's manuscript from which they must ultimately derive.

For a long time, no systematic attempts were made to correct Shakespeare's texts. In reprints of the quartos, which went on appearing during the seventeenth century, sporadic corrections of obvious misprints were made, but these texts have no independent authority. Nor do the reprints of the Folio of 1632, 1663, and 1685. The second issue (1664) of the third Folio was the first to include *Pericles*; it also added six apocryphal plays.

Only in the eighteenth century was a start made on the process of correcting the early texts and presenting them in newly attractive and helpful ways. In 1709 the playwright Nicholas Rowe issued an edition, in six volumes, which was prefaced by the first formal biography and illustrated with engravings. It was based on the Fourth Folio, with some consultation of quartos, but Rowe, like almost all subsequent editors, introduced modernizations of spelling and punctuation. His is the first edition to divide the plays systematically into acts and scenes, and to indicate locations for the scenes. He also made many necessary textual corrections. The process that Rowe began was continued and developed by many later editors with varying degrees of thoroughness and scholarship. For modern readers, editions from Rowe's to those of the mid-nineteenth century are of mainly historical interest, but it is worth remembering that during this period most of the standard emendations were made, and many explanatory annotations that are still current were first offered. Equally, many conventions of presentation were established, some of which continued to be adopted, often unthinkingly, by later editors. Rowe's successors included Alexander Pope (1723–5), Lewis Theobald (1733),

78

A page from the First Folio, 1623, including Hamlet's soliloquy, *O what a rogue* (II.ii). *Photograph University of London Library*

So as a painted Tyrant *Pyrrhus* stood,
And like a Newtrall to his will and matter, did nothing.
But as we often see against some storme,
A silence in the Heauens, the Racke stand still,
The bold windes speechlesse, and the Orbe below
As hush as death : Anon the dreadfull Thunder
Doth rend the Region. So after *Pyrrhus* pause,
A rowsed Vengeance sets him new a-worke,
And neuer did the Cyclops hammers fall
On Mars his Armours, forg'd for proofe Eterne,
With lesse remorse then *Pyrrhus* bleeding sword
Now falles on *Priam.*
Out, out, thou Strumpet-Fortune, all you Gods,
In generall Synod take away her power:
Breake all the Spokes and Fallies from her wheele,
And boule the round Naue downe the hill of Heauen,
As low as to the Fiends.
Pol. This is too long.
Ham. It shall to'th Barbars, with your beard. Pry-thee say on : He's for a Iigge, or a tale of Baudry, or hee sleepes. Say on; come to *Hecuba.*
1. *Play.* But who, O who, had seene the inobled Queen.
Ham. The inobled Queene?
Pol. That's good : Inobled Queene is good.
1. *Play.* Run bare-foot vp and downe,
Threatning the flame
With Bisson Rheume : A clout about that head,
Where late the Diadem stood, and for a Robe
About her lanke and all ore-teamed Loines,
A blanket in th'Alarum of feare caught vp.
Who this had seene, with tongue in Venome steep'd,
'Gainst Fortunes State, would Treason haue pronounc'd?
But if the Gods themselues did see her then,
When she saw *Pyrrhus* make malicious sport
In mincing with his Sword her Husbands limbes,
The instant Burst of Clamour that she made
(Vnlesse things mortall moue them not at all)
Would haue made milche the Burning eyes of Heauen,
And passion in the Gods.
Pol. Looke where he ha's not turn'd his colour, and ha's teares in's eyes. Pray you no more.
Ham. 'Tis well, Ile haue thee speake out the rest, soone. Good my Lord, will you see the Players wel be-stow'd. Do ye heare, let them be well vs'd : for they are the Abstracts and breefe Chronicles of the time. After your death, you were better haue a bad Epitaph, then their ill report while you liued.
Pol. My Lord, I will vse them according to their de-sart.
Ham. Gods bodykins man, better. Vse euerie man after his desart, and who should scape whipping : vse them after your own Honor and Dignity. The lesse they deserue, the more merit is in your bountie. Take them in.
Pol. Come sirs. *Exit Polon.*
Ham. Follow him Friends: wee'l heare a play to mor-row. Dost thou heare me old Friend, can you play the murther of *Gonzago?*
Play. I my Lord.
Ham. Wee'l ha't to morrow night. You could for a need study a speech of some dosen or sixteene lines, which I would set downe, and insert in't? Could ye not?
Play. I my Lord.
Ham. Very well. Follow that Lord, and looke you mock him not. My good Friends, Ile leaue you til night you are welcome to *Elsonower?*

Rosin. Good my Lord. *Exeunt.*
Manet Hamlet.
Ham. I so, God buy'ye : Now I am alone.
Oh what a Rogue and Pesant slaue am I?
Is it not monstrous that this Player heere,
But in a Fixion, in a dreame of Passion,
Could force his soule so to his whole conceit,
That from her working, all his visage warm'd;
Teares in his eyes, distraction in's Aspect,
A broken voyce, and his whole Function suiting
With Formes, to his Conceit? And all for nothing?
For *Hecuba?*
What's *Hecuba* to him, or he to *Hecuba,*
That he should weepe for her? What would he doe,
Had he the Motiue and the Cue for passion
That I haue? He would drowne the Stage with teares,
And cleaue the generall eare with horrid speech:
Make mad the guilty, and apale the free,
Confound the ignorant, and amaze indeed,
The very faculty of Eyes and Eares. Yet I,
A dull and muddy-metled Rascall, peake
Like Iohn a-dreames, vnpregnant of my cause,
And can say nothing : No, not for a King,
Vpon whose property, and most deere life,
A damn'd defeate was made. Am I a Coward?
Who calles me Villaine? breakes my pate a-crosse?
Pluckes off my Beard, and blowes it in my face?
Tweakes me by'th'Nose? giues me the Lye i'th'Throate,
As deepe as to the Lungs? Who does me this?
Ha? Why I should take it : for it cannot be,
But I am Pigeon-Liuer'd, and lacke Gall
To make Oppression bitter, or ere this,
I should haue fatted all the Region Kites
With this Slaues Offall, bloudy : a Bawdy villaine,
Remorselesse, Treacherous, Letcherous, kindles villaine!
Oh Vengeance!
Who? What an Asse am I? I sure, this is most braue,
That I, the Sonne of the Deere murthered,
Prompted to my Reuenge by Heauen, and Hell,
Must (like a Whore) vnpacke my heart with words,
And fall a Cursing like a very Drab.
A Scullion? Fye vpon't : Foh. About my Braine.
I haue heard, that guilty Creatures sitting at a Play,
Haue by the very cunning of the Scoene,
Bene strooke so to the soule, that presently
They haue proclaim'd their Malefactions.
For Murther, though it haue no tongue, will speake
With most myraculous Organ. Ile haue these Players,
Play something like the murder of my Father,
Before mine Vnkle. Ile obserue his lookes,
Ile tent him to the quicke : If he but blench
I know my course. The Spirit that I haue seene
May be the Diuell, and the Diuel hath power
T'assume a pleasing shape, yea and perhaps
Out of my Weaknesse, and my Melancholly,
As he is very potent with such Spirits,
Abuses me to damne me. Ile haue grounds
More Relatiue then this: The Play's the thing,
Wherein Ile catch the Conscience of the King. *Exit*

Enter King, Queene, Polonius, Ophelia, Ro-sincrance, Guildenstern, and Lords.

King. And can you by no drift of circumstance
Get from him why he puts on this Confusion:
Grating so harshly all his dayes of quiet
With

THE
CRONICLE
Hiſtory of Henry the fift,

With his battell fought at *Agin Court* in
France. Togither with *Auntient*
Piſtoll.

As it hath bene ſundry times playd by the Right honorable
the Lord Chamberlaine his ſeruants.

LONDON

Printed by *Thomas Creede,* for Tho. Milling-
ton, and Iohn Busby. And are to be
ſold at his houſe in Carter Lane, next
the Powle head. 1600.

The title-page of *Henry V,* 1600, one of the 'bad quartos'. *Photograph*
University of London Library.

Sir Thomas Hanmer (1743-4), William Warburton (1747), Samuel Johnson (1765), whose Preface and notes put him among the great Shakespeare critics, Edward Capell (1767-8), George Steevens (1773, 1778, 1785, 1793), and Edmond Malone (1790). Much of the scholarship of these editors was brought together in the second edition of Malone, completed by James Boswell the younger, published in 1823, and sometimes called the Third Variorum. (The First Variorum (1803) was Isaac Reed's, based on Steevens, the Second an 1813 reprint of this.)

Of the many complete editions that appeared during the nineteenth century, the most important is the nine-volume Cambridge Shakespeare (1863-1866, revised 1891-1893), edited by W. G. Clark, J. Glover, and W. A. Wright, for many years the standard text, especially in the single-volume, Globe version of 1864. In 1871 appeared the first volume of the American New Variorum, a play-by-play edition edited originally by H. H. Furness which is still in progress. W. J. Craig's Oxford edition dates from 1891, and the 37 volumes of the original Arden edition were published from 1899 to 1924.

At the beginning of the twentieth century a revolution in textual studies greatly advanced understanding of the bases of Shakespeare's text, and transformed attitudes to the editing of his works. A number of important editions have resulted. The New Shakespeare (1921-1966), edited by J. Dover Wilson and others, has valuable notes and other material, but is textually eccentric. G. L. Kittredge's (1936, revised in 1970) has a reliable text and excellent notes. Peter Alexander's unannotated one-volume edition (1951) is often used for reference, though it follows the line-numbering of the Globe. Hardin Craig's annotated text (1951) has been popular in America. In 1951 a new Arden began to appear, a one-play-per-volume series, with detailed annotation, which in general is now regarded as the standard edition for scholarly purposes. It is still incomplete. C. J. Sisson's one-volume edition (1954) has useful introductions and appendices. The Pelican (1956-67) and Signet (1963-68) lightly annotated paperback editions have been reprinted as hardback single volumes; the New Penguin (1967-) offers fuller annotation and more extended introductions. The Riverside edition (1974), under the General Editorship of G. Blakemore Evans, has an over-conservative text, but otherwise its wealth of ancillary material makes it the ideal desert-island Shakespeare.

There is no end to the editing of Shakespeare, partly because an infinite number of solutions can be offered to the problems posed by his text, partly because different methods of presentation and annotation are required for an ever-changing readership, and a little because of advances in scholarship. No satisfactory old-spelling edition has appeared, but those wishing to read the texts as they were originally printed are well served by *The Norton Facsimile of The First Folio of Shakespeare*, prepared by Charlton Hinman (1968), and by the Shakespeare Quarto Facsimiles, edited by W. W. Greg and, later, Charlton Hinman (1939–).

VIII. SHAKESPEARE IN PERFORMANCE

We know little about performances of Shakespeare's plays during the years immediately following his death. Court performances are recorded, and it is clear that some, at least, of the plays remained in the regular repertory of the King's Men. The closing of the theatres in 1642, when Cromwell came to power, is the most decisive break in the history of the English stage. When they re-opened, in 1660, conditions changed greatly. The new buildings resembled the closed, private theatres of the earlier period rather than the open, public ones. Women took over the boys' roles. Some of Shakespeare's plays, especially the romantic comedies, were not revived. Patents were given to only two companies, and the plays were distributed between them. Some, such as *Hamlet, Othello,* and *Julius Caesar,* continued to be performed in versions which, if abbreviated, were not substantially altered. Others were radically adapted both to suit the new conditions and to conform to changes in taste. Sir William Davenant (1606–68), who boasted of being Shakespeare's

Sarah Siddons as Lady Macbeth; an engraving by R. Cooper, 1822, from the portrait by G. H. Harlow. *By Courtesy of the Victoria and Albert Museum (Theatre Museum), Crown copyright.*

natural son and who had written for the Caroline stage, led one of the new companies, for which he adapted *Macbeth* (1663) and combined parts of *Measure for Measure* and *Much Ado About Nothing* to make *The Law Against Lovers* (1662). He collaborated with the young John Dryden on an adaptation of *The Tempest* as *The Enchanted Isle* (1667; further revised as an opera by Thomas Shadwell, in 1673). Dryden himself adapted *Troilus and Cressida* (1679); Nahum Tate, *King Lear* (1681); and Colley Cibber, *Richard III* (1699). The *Macbeth* had singing, dancing and flying witches, additional scenes for the women characters, and a moralistic dying speech for Macbeth. *The Enchanted Isle* added sisters for both Miranda and Caliban, balanced Ferdinand with Hippolito, who has never seen a woman, added a female sprite, and greatly increased the play's spectacular appeal. Tate introduced into *King Lear* a love affair between Edgar and Cordelia, omitted the Fool, and sent Lear, Gloucester and Kent into peaceful retirement. Cibber greatly shortened *Richard III*, altered its structure, added passages from other plays, omitted important characters, and increased the relative length of Richard's role. All these authors rewrote and added speeches. Their adaptations, and others like them, are important because they kept the original plays off the stage, some of them well into the nineteenth century. Cibber's influence extends even as far as Olivier's film (1955).

The greatest actor on the Restoration stage was Thomas Betterton (c. 1635–1710), who played many of the principal Shakespearian roles, most notably Hamlet. No-one of comparable stature emerged until David Garrick (1717–78) made his sensational London debut in Cibber's *Richard III* in 1741. He excelled in roles as varied as Benedick, Richard III, Hamlet, Romeo, King Lear, and Macbeth. Though he restored Shakespeare's language in some passages of the adaptations, he made new versions of *The Taming of the Shrew* (as *Catharine and Petruchio*, 1756), *The Winter's Tale* (as *Florizel and Perdita*, 1756) and *Hamlet* (1772). His great admiration was largely instrumental in establishing the reverential attitude to Shakespeare as England's major classic author, and the Jubilee which Garrick organized at Stratford-upon-Avon in 1769 was the first large-scale celebration.

Edmund Kean as Othello: an engraving by W. Sheldricks from the portrait by E. Lambert. Kean first played the part in 1814. *By courtesy of the Victoria and Albert Museum (Theatre Museum), Crown Copyright*

This attitude intensified during the Romantic period. Like Garrick, John Philip Kemble (1757–1823) was important as actor, manager, and, to a lesser extent, play reviser. He and his sister, Sarah Siddons (1755–1831), were classical performers, he impressive as Hamlet, Brutus, and Coriolanus, she as Volumnia, Constance, and, supremely, Lady Macbeth. Far different was Edmund Kean (1787–1833), volatile and electrifying as Shylock, Richard III, Hamlet, and Othello.

Objections to the standard adaptations were increasingly voiced, and among the earliest to put them into practice was William Charles Macready (1793–1873), who in 1838 restored Shakespeare's *King Lear*. But the performances of the greatest integrity since the early seventeenth century seem to be those of Samuel Phelps (1804–1878), the actor-manager who presented all but six of Shakespeare's plays at Sadler's Wells from 1844 to 1862. Increasingly during the nineteenth century attention was paid to visual effect. With Macready and Phelps it was controlled with discretion and taste, but Charles Kean (1811–68), whose major productions were given at the Princess's from 1850 to 1859, sacrificed textual integrity and even theatrical excitement to pictorialism and archaeological verisimilitude. Sir Henry Irving (1838–1905) was a far finer actor as well as the successful manager of the Lyceum.

Reaction against the spectacular tradition began effectively with the work of William Poel (1852–1934), whose productions with the Elizabethan Stage Society (founded in 1894), though textually impure, attempted with some success to return to Elizabethan staging methods, and so opened the way for performances in which better texts could be played without rearrangements necessitated by scene-changing. He worked with Harley Granville Barker (1877–1946), whose productions at the Savoy from 1912 to 1914 showed that it was possible to combine textual integrity with scenic appeal.

The period between the two World Wars included much experimentation, as in the modern-dress productions of Sir Barry Jackson (1879–1961), Sir Tyrone Guthrie (1900–1971), and others, though disciples of William Poel such as Robert Atkins (1886–1972), W. Bridges-Adams (1889–1965) and B. Iden-Payne (1881–1976) directed performances in a

86

Laurence Olivier as Hotspur in the Old Vic production of *Henry IV, Part One*, 1945 *John Vickers Archive*

more traditional style. Gradually directors increased in importance, though Sir Donald Wolfit (1902–1968) continued the tradition of the actor-manager, and major players, including Dame Sybil Thorndike (1882–1976), Dame Edith Evans (1888–1976), Sir John Gielgud, and Sir Laurence (later Lord) Olivier, distinguished themselves in Shakespearian roles at the Old Vic, the Stratford Memorial Theatre, and elsewhere.

The dominance of the director increased still further after the Second World War, with the work of Peter Brook, Peter Hall, John Barton, and Trevor Nunn, all of whom have worked at what is now the Royal Shakespeare Theatre, Stratford-upon-Avon, which, since the closure of the Old Vic in 1963, has become the main centre of Shakespearian production in England, though important performances have been given at the National Theatre, and by many other companies.

Shakespeare belongs, of course, to far more than the English stage. Books by Charles Shattuck and Robert Speaight listed in the bibliography tell something of the story of his popularity in American and Continental theatres. Annual festivals at Ashland, Oregon; Stratford, Connecticut; Stratford, Ontario; and in Central Park, New York present his work to the great American public. All over the world, the plays are enjoyed in many languages, and through the media of radio, television, cinema, and the gramophone as well as the stage. Shakespeare's wooden O has become the great globe itself.

IX. SHAKESPEARE'S CRITICS

Critical comment on Shakespeare by his contemporaries is limited to scattered remarks such as Meres's empty eulogy (p. 37), William Drummond of Hawthornden's reports of Ben Jonson's informal conversation, and the tributes printed in the First Folio. For a century or more after this, most comment is of a general nature, and much of it tells us more

89

Judi Dench as Viola in John Barton's Royal Skakespeare Company production of *Twelfth Night*, 1969. *Holte Photographics* about the taste of the time than about Shakespeare. John Dryden wrote the first important criticism, mainly in the *Essay of Dramatic Poesy* (1688), the *Essay on the Dramatic Poetry of the Last Age* (1672), and the Preface to *Troilus and Cressida* (1679), his adaptation of Shakespeare's play. Though he found that 'the fury of his fancy often transported him beyond the bounds of judgement, either in coining of new words and phrases, or racking words which were in use, into the violence of a catachresis', he praised Shakespeare nobly as 'the man who of all modern and, perhaps, ancient poets had the largest and most comprehensive soul'. Thomas Rymer's notoriously destructive criticism of *Othello* comes in his *Short View of Tragedy* (1693).

During the eighteenth century, editions of the plays provided an outlet for opinion. Dryden's view that Shakespeare's greatness lies in his successful imitation of nature persisted. Alexander Pope, in his Preface (1725), wrote 'His characters are so much nature herself that 'tis a sort of injury to call them by so distant a name as copies of her.' Dr Johnson, in his magisterial Preface and in the pithy notes to his edition (1765), enumerated both Shakespeare's faults and his merits. He found Shakespeare's morality unsatisfying: 'He sacrifices virtue to convenience, and is so much more careful to please than to instruct, that he seems to write without any moral purpose.' But he also praised Shakespeare as 'the poet that holds up to his readers a faithful mirror of manners and of life'.

During the later part of the century there developed a fascination with Shakespeare's characters as independent creations, evinced in William Richardson's *Philosophical Analysis of Some of Shakespeare's Remarkable Characters* (1774) and Maurice Morgann's fine *Essay on the Dramatic Character of Sir John Falstaff* (1794), which is romantic in its imaginative identification with the character. Walter Whiter's *Specimen of a Commentary on Shakespeare* (1794) anticipates some of the imagery criticism of the twentieth century.

German interest developed early, and August Wilhelm Schlegel probably influenced Samuel Taylor Coleridge whose detailed appreciations, seminal in their effect, have to be retrieved from a multitude of sources, including notebooks, marginalia, and other people's reports of his lectures. Coleridge encouraged a reverential submission to Shakespeare, finding that the plays have their own organic unity. William Hazlitt's eulogistic *Characters of Shakespear's Plays* (1817), based in part on his theatre reviews, reveals a preoccupation with dramatic character which reflects the nature of performances in an age of great acting. Keen theatregoer though he was, Hazlitt shared some of the sentiments that Charles Lamb expressed in his essay 'On the Tragedies of Shakespeare Considered with Reference to their Fitness for Stage Representation' (1811), in which he argued that the plays suffer in performance. The mid-nineteenth century produced little distinguished Shakespeare criticism, but its later decades saw an increase in scholarly interest which, along with the establishment of English studies as a University discipline, greatly increased the amount of serious writing on Shakespeare. Edward Dowden's *Shakspere: His Mind and Art* (1875) is a thoughtful study of Shakespeare's development which has had deserved popularity. Much of Bernard Shaw's brilliant, sometimes iconoclastic criticism is found in the reviews of performances written for the *Saturday Review* from 1895 to 1898. Far different is A. C. Bradley's sensitive, scrupulous, philosophical study *Shakespearean Tragedy* (1904), limited to *Hamlet, Othello, King Lear,* and *Macbeth*, which is in some respects a culmination of earlier interest in character portrayal.

A reaction against this is found in the work of E. E. Stoll and L. L. Schücking, both of whom sought a more objective approach, insisting that Shakespeare should be considered in the context of his life and the literary conventions of his age. Stoll, in his many writings, asserted the importance of poetry, and the primacy of plot over character. Harley Granville-Barker, in his series of Prefaces to individual plays, published from 1927 to 1947, usefully discussed them in terms of the problems and opportunities with which they confront their performers.

In the 1930s, the dominance of a school of criticism concerned with close verbal analysis precipitated language-based studies such as Caroline Spurgeon's pioneering *Shakespeare's Imagery and What it Tells Us* (1935), Wolfgang H. Clemen's

The Development of Shakespeare's Imagery (1936, translated 1951), and the many books of G. Wilson Knight, a verbal critic of great subtlety who has added to our understanding of Shakespeare's symbolism and, more generally, of his imaginative processes. From among the critics of more recent years it is difficult to distinguish equally dominant figures. This may be because we lack historical perspective, but may also reflect the increasing fragmentation of critical approaches to Shakespeare. The bibliography appended to this essay lists important studies of the sources and of the literary and dramatic background by, among others, W. W. Lawrence, M. C. Bradbrook, Geoffrey Bullough, Kenneth Muir, Anne Righter, and Emrys Jones; of the historical background by Hardin Craig, Lily B. Campbell, and E. M. W. Tillyard; writings showing a particular concern with Shakespeare's social environment, by S. L. Bethell and Alfred Harbage; theatrically based studies by Arthur Colby Sprague, Nevill Coghill, John Russell Brown, Marvin Rosenberg, and Joseph G. Price; ones based on psycho-analytical procedures, by J. I. M. Stewart and Ernest Jones; others grounded in moral preoccupations, by Derek Traversi, L. C. Knights, and Arthur Sewell; some with an anthropo-logical basis, by Northrop Frye, C. L. Barber, and John Holloway; and examples of close stylistic analysis by M. M. Mahood, Harry Levin, and Maurice Charney. Most of these critics, and others, are, to a greater or lesser degree, eclectic in their methods. Shakespeare continues to stimulate, not merely professional diploma pieces, but challenging criticism, because his works remain alive as an intellectual and imagina-tive force, constantly creating newly fruitful relationships between themselves and those who experience them whether in the theatre or on the page. So long as they are enjoyed, there will be something new to be said about them.

BIBLIOGRAPHY

The bibliography is, necessarily, highly selective. Individual essays, which often contain good criticism, are omitted; they, along with other items, may be traced through the bibliographies listed in the opening section, and through the annual bibliographies, critical surveys, and reviews in the Shakespeare periodicals. Reprints are not listed.

1. BIBLIOGRAPHIES

Shakespeare Bibliography: A Dictionary of Every Known Issue of the Writings of our National Poet and of Recorded Opinion Thereon in the English Language, William Jaggard, Stratford-upon-Avon, 1911.

A Shakespeare Bibliography, W. Ebisch and L. L. Schücking. Oxford, 1931; *Supplement for the Years 1930–35,* Oxford, 1937.

A Classified Shakespeare Bibliography, 1936–1958, Gordon Ross Smith, Pennsylvania, 1963.

A Reader's Guide to Shakespeare's Plays, Ronald S. Berman, Chicago, Ill., 1965; rev. 1973.

Shakespeare: Select Bibliographical Guides, ed. Stanley Wells, Oxford, 1973.

A Selective Bibliography of Shakespeare, James G. McManaway and Jeanne Addison Roberts, Charlottesville, Va., 1975.

2. COLLECTED EDITIONS

ed. W. G. Clark, W. A. Wright, and J. Glover, 9 vols., London, 1863–6, 2nd edn., 1867, 3rd edn., revised by Wright, 1891–3 (the Cambridge Shakespeare, on which the Globe (1864) was based).

ed. H. H. Furness, Jr., and others, Philadelphia, Pa.. 1871–1928; New York, 1929– (the New Variorum).

ed. C. F. Tucker Brooke, *The Shakespeare Apocrypha,* Oxford, 1918.

ed. J. Dover Wilson, Sir A. T. Quiller-Couch, and others, Cambridge, 1921–66 (the New Shakespeare).

ed. G. L. Kittredge, Boston, Mass., 1936.

ed. W. W. Greg and Charlton Hinman, *Shakespeare Quarto Fascimiles,* London, 1939–52; Oxford, 1957–.

ed. Peter Alexander, London and Glasgow, 1951.

ed. Hardin Craig, Chicago, Ill., 1951.

ed. U. Ellis-Fermor, Harold F. Brooks, Harold Jenkins, and Brian Morris, London, 1951 (the new Arden).

ed. C. J. Sisson, London, 1954.

ed. Alfred Harbage (general editor), Baltimore, Md., 1956–67; one-volume edn., 1969 (the Pelican).

ed. Sylvan Barnet (general editor), New York, 1963–68; one-volume edn., 1972 (the Signet).

Shakespeare's Poems . . . A Facsimile of the Earliest Editions, with a Preface by Louis M. Martz and Eugene M. Waith, New Haven, Conn., 1964.
ed. T. J. B. Spencer (general editor), Harmondsworth, 1967– (the New Penguin).
ed. Charlton Hinman, *The First Folio of Shakespeare,* New York, 1968 (facsimile).
ed. G. Blakemore Evans, Boston, Mass., 1974 (the Riverside).

3. TEXTUAL STUDIES

Shakespeare Folios and Quartos: A Study in the Bibliography of Shakespeare's Plays 1594–1685, A. W. Pollard, London, 1909.
Shakespeare's Fight with the Pirates and the Problems of the Transmission of his Text, A. W. Pollard, London, 1917; 2nd edn., Cambridge, 1920.
The Editorial Problem in Shakespeare: A Survey of the Foundations of the Text, W. W. Greg, Oxford, 1943; rev. 1951, 1954.
Textual Problems of the First Folio; 'Richard III,' 'King Lear', 'Troilus and Cressida', '2 Henry IV', 'Othello', Alice Walker, Cambridge, 1953.
The Shakespeare First Folio: Its Bibliographical and Textual History, D. W. Greg, Oxford, 1955.
New Readings in Shakespeare, C. J. Sisson, 2 vols., Cambridge, 1956.
The Printing and Proof-Reading of the First Folio of Shakespeare, Charlton Hinman, 2 vols., Oxford, 1963.
The Stability of Shakespeare's Text, E. A. J. Honigmann, London, 1965.
On Editing Shakespeare and the Elizabethan Dramatists, Fredson Bowers, Pennsylvania, 1955; 2nd edn., Charlottesville, Va., 1966.

4. REFERENCE WORKS AND PERIODICALS

Shakespeare Jahrbuch, West, Vols. 1–99, Berlin, 1865–1963; vols. 100– , Heidelberg, 1964– .
A Shakespearian Grammer, E. A. Abbott, London, 1869, rev. 1871.
Shakespeare-Lexicon, Alexander Schmidt, 2 vols., Berlin, 1874–75; rev. G. Sarrazin, 4th edn., Berlin, 1923.
A Shakespeare Glossary, C. T. Onions, Oxford, 1911.
A Dictionary of the Characters and Proper Names in the Works of Shakespeare, F. G. Stokes, London, 1924.
A Topographical Dictionary to the Works of Shakespeare and his Fellow Dramatists, E. H. Sugden, Manchester, 1925.
Shakespeare's Bawdy: A Literary and Psychological Essay and a Comprehensive Glossary, Eric Partridge, London, 1947, rev. 1968.
Shakespeare Survey, Cambrdige, 1948– .
Shakespeare Quarterly, New York, 1950–72; Washington, D.C., 1972.
Shakespeare's Characters: A Historical Dictionary, W. H. Thomson, Altrincham, 1951.

A Shakespeare Companion 1550–1950, F. E. Halliday, London, 1952; rev. as *A Shakespeare Companion 1564–1964*, Harmondsworth, 1964.

Shakespeare's Names: A Pronouncing Dictionary, Helge Kökeritz, New Haven, Conn., 1959.

Shakespeare Jahrbuch, East, Weimar, 1965– .

Shakespeare Studies, vols. 1–2, Cincinnati, Ohio, 1965–67; vols. 4–6, Dubuque, Iowa, 1968–70; vol. 7–, Columbia, S.C., 1974; vols. 8–, New York, 1975– .

The Reader's Encyclopaedia of Shakespeare, Oscar James Campbell and Edward G. Quinn, New York, 1966.

The Vocal Songs in the Plays of Shakespeare, Peter J. Seng, Cambridge, Mass., 1967.

A Complete and Systematic Concordance to the Works of Shakespeare, Marvin Spevack, Hildesheim, 1968–70; *The Harvard Concordance to Shakespeare*, Marvin Spevack, Cambridge, Mass., 1973.

A New Companion to Shakespeare Studies, ed. Kenneth Muir and S. Schoenbaum, Cambridge, 1971.

Shakespeare: An Illustrated Dictionary, Stanley Wells, London and New York, 1978.

5. BIOGRAPHICAL STUDIES

William Shakespeare; A Study of Facts and Problems, Sir Edmund K. Chambers, 2 vols, Oxford, 1930; abridged by Charles Williams as *A Short Life of Shakespeare with the Sources*, Oxford, 1933.

Shakespeare versus Shallow, Leslie Hotson, Boston, Mass., 1931.

The Essential Shakespeare; A Biographical Adventure, J. Dover Wilson, Cambridge, 1932.

I, William Shakespeare, Leslie Hotson, London, 1937.

Shakespeare, Man and Artist, Edgar I. Fripp, 2 vols., Oxford, 1938.

William Shakspere's Petty School, T. W. Baldwin, Urbana, Ill., 1943.

William Shakspere's Small Latine and Lesse Greeke, 2 vols., T. W. Baldwin, Urbana, Ill., 1944.

Shakespeare's Sonnets Dated; and Other Essays, Leslie Hotson, Oxford, 1949.

Shakespeare; His World and His Work, M. M. Reese, London, 1953.

Shakespeare As Collaborator, Kenneth Muir, London, 1960.

Shakespeare; A Biographical Handbook, Gerald Eades Bentley, New Haven, Conn., 1961.

Shakespeare in Warwickshire, Mark Eccles, Madison, Wisc., 1961.

Shakespeare, Peter Quennell, London, 1963.

Shakespeare, Peter Alexander, Oxford, 1964.

Shakespeare's Lives, S. Schoenbaum, Oxford, 1970.

Shakespeare; A Documentary Life, S. Schoenbaum, Oxford, 1975; Compact edn., 1977.

Shakespeare: The Man and his Achievement, Robert Speaight, London, 1977.

6. REPUTATION AND HISTORY OF CRITICISM

Shakespeare in the Eighteenth Century, D. Nichol Smith, Oxford, 1928.
A History of Shakespearian Criticism, A. Ralli, 2 vols, Oxford, 1932.
The Shakespeare Allusion-Book, J. Munro, rev. by Sir Edmund K. Chambers, 2 vols., Oxford, 1932.
Shakespeare and Jonson: Their Reputations in the Seventeenth Century Compared, 2 vols., Gerald Eades Bentley, Chicago, Ill., 1945.
His Exits and his Entrances: the Story of Shakespeare's Reputation, Louis Marder, Philadelphia, Pa., 1963.
Shakespeare in Europe, ed. Oswald LeWinter, Cleveland, Ohio, 1963.
Conceptions of Shakespeare, Alfred Harbage, Cambridge, Mass., 1966.
A Short History of Shakespearean Criticism, Arthur M. Eastman, New York, 1968.
Shakespeare: The Critical Heritage, ed. Brian Vickers, vol. 1, 1623–1692, London, 1974; vol. 2, 1693–1733, London, 1974; vol. 3, 1733–1752, London, 1975; vol. 4, 1753–1765, London, 1976, etc.

7. SOURCES, INFLUENCES, AND BACKGROUND STUDIES

Shakespeare and Music, Edward W. Naylor, London, 1896, rev. 1931.
The Diary of Master William Silence: A Study of Shakespeare and of Elizabethan Sport, D. H. Madden, London, 1897, rev. 1907.
Shakespeare's England: An Account of the Life and Manners of his Age, ed. Sir Sidney Lee and C. T. Onions, 2 vols., Oxford, 1916.
Shakespeare's Use of Song, Richmond Noble, London, 1923, rev. 1931.
Shakespeare's Biblical Knowledge and Use of the Book of Common Prayer, Richmond Noble, London, 1935.
Costume in the Drama of Shakespeare and his Contemporaries, M. C. Linthicum, Oxford, 1936.
The Enchanted Glass: The Elizabethan Mind in Literature, Hardin Craig, Oxford, 1936.
Shakespeare's Philosophical Patterns, W. C. Curry, Baton Rouge, La., 1937.
The Elizabethan World Picture, E. M. W. Tillyard, London, 1943.
Shakespeare and the Romance Tradition, E. C. Pettet, London, 1949.
Shakespeare's Heraldry, C. W. Scott-Giles, London, 1950.
The Little World of Man, J. B. Bamborough, London, 1952.
Shakespeare and the Classics, J. A. K. Thomson, London, 1952.
Marlowe and the Early Shakespeare, F. P. Wilson, Oxford, 1953.
Shakespeare's Use of Learning, Virgil K. Whitaker, San Marino, Calif., 1953.
Shakespeare's Military World, Paul A. Jorgensen, Berkeley, Calif., 1956.
Narrative and Dramatic Sources of Shakespeare, ed. Geoffrey Bullough, 8 vols. London, 1957–75.
The Anatomy of Puck, K. M. Briggs, London, 1959.

Shakespeare and the Artist, W. Moelwyn Merchant, Oxford, 1959.
Pale Hecate's Team, K. M. Briggs, London, 1962.
Music in Shakespearian Tragedy, F. W. Sternfeld, London, 1963.
Shakespeare and Christian Doctrine, R. Mushat Frye, Princeton, N.J., 1963.
Shakespeare's Plutarch, ed. T. J. B. Spencer, Harmondsworth, 1964.
Shakespeare in Music, ed. Phyllis Hartnoll, London, 1964.
Shakespeare and the Sea, A. F. Falconer, London, 1964.
Shakespeare's Legal and Political Background, George W. Keeton, London, 1967.
Shakespeare and the Classical Tradition: A Critical Guide to Commentary, John W. Velz, Minneapolis, Minn., 1968.
Elizabethan Love Stories, ed. T. J. B. Spencer, Harmondsworth, 1968.
Shakespeare's Holinshed, ed. Richard Hosley, New York, 1968.
Shakespeare and the Greek Romance, Carol Gesner, Lexington, Ky., 1970.
Shakespeare's Religious Background, Peter C. Milward, London, 1973.
The Dramatic Use of Bawdy in Shakespeare, E. A. C. Colman, London, 1974.
The Origins of Shakespeare, Emrys Jones, Oxford, 1977.
Shakespeare's Sources, Kenneth Muir, London, 1977.

8. LANGUAGE AND STYLE

A Specimen of a Commentary on Shakespeare (1794), Walter Whiter, ed. Alan Over and Mary Bell, London, 1967.
Shakespeare's Imagery and What It Tells Us, Caroline F. E. Spurgeon, Cambridge, 1935.
Shakespeare and the Arts of Language, Sister Miriam Joseph, New York, 1947.
The Development of Shakespeare's Imagery, Wolfgang H. Clemen, London, 1951, rev. 1977.
The Language of Shakespeare's Plays, B. Ifor Evans, London, 1952.
Explorations in Shakespeare's Language: Some Problems of Lexical Meaning in the Dramatic Text, Hilda M. Hulme, London, 1962.
The Artistry of Shakespeare's Prose, Brian Vickers, London, 1968.
The Language of Shakespeare, G. L. Brook, London, 1976.

9. SHAKESPEARE'S THEATRE

The Elizabethan Stage, Sir Edmund K. Chambers, 4 vols., Oxford, 1923.
Shakespeare's Audience, Alfred Harbage, New York, 1941.
Shakespeare's Globe Playhouse: A Modern Reconstruction, Irwin Smith, New York, 1956.
Shakespeare's Wooden O, Leslie Hotson, London, 1959.
Acting Shakespeare, Bertram Joseph, London, 1960.
Shakespeare at the Globe: 1599–1609, Bernard Beckerman, New York, 1962.
Shakespeare's Blackfriars Playhouse: Its History and Design, Irwin Smith, New York, 1964.

Shakespeare's Stagecraft, J. L. Styan, Cambridge, 1967.
The Globe Restored, C. Walter Hodges, London, 1953; 2nd edn., Oxford, 1968.
The Shakespearian Stage, 1571–1642, Andrew Gurr, Cambridge, 1970.

10. SHAKESPEARE IN THE POST-RESTORATION THEATRE

Shakespeare—from Betterton to Irving, George C. D. Odell, 2 vols., New York, 1920.
Shakespeare Improved: the Restoration Versions in Quarto and on the Stage, Hazelton Spencer, Cambridge, Mass., 1927.
Shakespeare and the Actors: The Stage Business in his Plays, 1660–1905, Arthur Colby Sprague, Cambridge, Mass., 1944.
Shakespeare in the Theatre 1701–1800, C. B. Hogan, 2 vols., Oxford, 1952–7.
Shakespearian Players and Performances, Arthur Colby Sprague, Cambridge, Mass., 1953.
Shakespeare on the English Stage 1900–1964, J. C. Trewin, London, 1964.
Shakespearian Production: with Especial Reference to the Tragedies, G. Wilson Knight, London, 1964.
Five Restoration Adaptations of Shakespeare, ed. Christopher Spencer, Urbana, Ill., 1965.
The Shakespeare Promptbooks: A Descriptive Catalogue, Charles H. Shattuck, Urbana, Ill., 1965.
Shakespeare's Plays in Performance, John Russell Brown, London, 1966.
Eyewitnesses of Shakespeare: First-Hand Accounts of Performances, 1590–1890, ed. Gāmini Salgādo, London, 1975.
Shakespeare on the American Stage, from the Hallams to Edwin Booth, Charles H. Shattuck, Washington, D.C., 1976.
Shakespeare on the Stage: An Illustrated History of Shakespearian Performance, Robert Speaight, London, 1973.
The Shakespeare Revolution, J. L. Styan, Cambridge, 1977.
Royal Shakespeare: Four major productions at Stratford-upon-Avon, Stanley Wells, Manchester, 1977.

11. GENERAL CRITICAL STUDIES

The Characters of Shakespear's Plays, William Hazlitt, 1817, etc.
Shakspere: A Critical Study of his Mind and Art, Edward Dowden, London, 1875.
Eighteenth-Century Essays on Shakespeare, ed. D. Nichol Smith, Glasgow, 1903; rev. Oxford, 1963.
Oxford Lectures on Poetry, A. C. Bradley, London, 1909.
Character Problems in Shakespeare's Plays, L. L. Schücking, London, 1922.
Shakespeare Studies, Historical and Comparative in Method, Elmer Edgar Stoll, New York, 1927.

Prefaces to Shakespeare, Harley Granville-Barker, 5 vols., London, 1927–47.

Coleridge's Shakespearian Criticism, ed. T. M. Raysor, 2 vols., London, 1930, rev. London, 1960.

The Wheel of Fire, G. Wilson Knight, Oxford, 1930, rev. London, 1949.

The Imperial Theme, G. Wilson Knight, Oxford, 1931.

The Shakespearian Tempest, G. Wilson Knight, Oxford, 1932.

Art and Artifice in Shakespeare: A Study in Dramatic Contrast and Illusion, Elmer Edgar Stoll, Cambridge, 1933.

Shakespeare, J. Middleton Murry, London, 1936.

Shakespeare's Young Lovers, Elmer Edgar Stoll, Oxford, 1937.

Shakespeare, Mark van Doren, London, 1939.

Shakespeare and Other Masters, Elmer Edgar Stoll, Cambridge, Mass., 1940.

Shakespeare's Satire, Oscar James Campbell, London, 1943.

Shakespeare and the Popular Dramatic Tradition, S. L. Bethell, London, 1944.

Elizabethan and Jacobean, F. P. Wilson, Oxford, 1945.

Shakespeare's Imagination: A Study of the Psychology of Association and Inspiration, E. A. Armstrong, London, 1946; rev. Gloucester, Mass., 1963.

As They Liked It: An Essay on Shakespeare and Morality, Alfred Harbage, New York, 1947.

A Notebook on William Shakespeare, Dame Edith Sitwell, London, 1948.

Character and Motive in Shakespeare: Some Recent Appraisals Examined, J. I. M. Stewart, London, 1949.

Character and Society in Shakespeare, Arthur Sewell, Oxford, 1951.

The Meaning of Shakespeare, Harold C. Goddard, 2 vols., Chicago, Ill., 1951.

Shakespeare and Elizabethan Poetry, M. C. Bradbrook, London, 1951.

Shakespeare and the Rival Traditions, Alfred Harbage, New York, 1952.

The Shakespearean Moment and its Place in the Poetry of the Seventeenth Century, Patrick Cruttwell, London, 1954.

The Sovereign Flower, G. Wilson Knight, London, 1958.

Some Shakespearian Themes, L. C. Knights, London, 1959.

Writings on Shakespeare, Samuel Taylor Coleridge, ed. Terence Hawkes, New York, 1959; repr. as *Coleridge on Shakespeare*, Harmondsworth, 1969.

Samuel Johnson on Shakespeare, ed. W. K. Wimsatt, New York, 1960; repr. as *Dr. Johnson on Shakespeare*, Harmondsworth, 1969.

Angel with Horns: and Other Shakespeare Lectures, A. P. Rossiter, London, 1961.

Early Shakespeare, ed. J. R. Brown and Bernard Harris (Stratford-upon-Avon Studies 3), London, 1961.

Shakespeare and the Idea of the Play, Anne Righter, London, 1962.

Shakespeare and the Nature of Man, Theodore Spencer, Cambridge, Mass., 1962.

Shaw on Shakespeare, ed. Edwin Wilson, London, 1962.

The Problem Plays of Shakespeare: A Study of 'Julius Caesar', 'Measure for Measure', 'Antony and Cleopatra', Ernest Schanzer, London, 1963.

Shakespeare Our Contemporary, Jan Kott, London, 1964, rev. 1967.

Shakespeare's Professional Skills, Nevill Coghill, London, 1964.

Dualities in Shakespeare, Marion B. North, Toronto, 1966.

Later Shakespeare, ed. J. R. Brown and Bernard Harris (Stratford-upon-Avon Studies 8), London, 1966.

The Early Shakespeare, A. C. Hamilton, San Marino, Calif., 1967.

Shakespeare and the Common Understanding, Norman Rabkin, New York, 1967.

Johnson on Shakespeare, ed. Arthur Sherbo, 2 vols. (Vols. 7 and 8 of the Yale edition of Samuel Johnson), New Haven, Conn., 1968.

Shakespeare and the Confines of Art, Philip Edwards, London, 1968.

Shakespeare the Craftsman, M. C. Bradbrook, London, 1969.

Shakespearian and Other Studies, F. P. Wilson, ed. Helen Gardner, Oxford, 1969.

Scenic Form in Shakespeare, Emrys Jones, Oxford, 1971.

Shakespeare's Metadrama, J. L. Calderwood, Minneapolis, Minn., 1971.

Shakespeare and the Energies of Drama, Michael Goldman, Princeton, N.J., 1972.

Shakespeare's Dramatic Art, Wolfgang H. Clemen, London, 1972.

Shakespeare the Professional and Related Studies, Kenneth Muir, London, 1973.

The Breath of Clowns and Kings: Shakespeare's Early Comedies and Histories, Theodore Weiss, New York, 1971.

The Heart's Forest: A Study of Shakespeare's Pastoral Plays, David P. Young, New Haven, Conn., 1972.

12. CRITICAL STUDIES OF THE COMEDIES

Shakespeare's Problem Comedies, W. W. Lawrence, New York, 1931.

A Study of 'Love's Labour's Lost', Frances Yates, Cambridge, 1936.

Comicall Satyre and Shakespeare's 'Troilus and Cressida', Oscar James Campbell, San Marino, Calif., 1938.

Shakespearian Comedy, H. B. Charlton, London, 1938.

Shakespearian Comedy and Other Studies, George Gordon, London, 1944.

The Love-Game Comedy, David Lloyd Stevenson, New York, 1946.

Moonlight at the Globe: An Essay in Shakespeare Production Based on Performance of 'A Midsummer Night's Dream' at Harrow School, Ronald Watkins, London, 1946.

The Crown of Life: Essays in Interpretation of Shakespeare's Final Plays, G. Wilson Knight, Oxford, 1947.

'The Winter's Tale': A Study, S. L. Bethell, London, 1947.

Shakespeare's Last Plays, E. M. W. Tillyard, London, 1948.

Shakespeare's Problem Plays, E. M. W. Tillyard, London, 1950.

Shakespearian Comedy, S. C. Sen Gupta, London, 1950.

Shakespeare's Motley, Leslie Hotson, London, 1952.

The Fool: His Social and Literary History, Enid Welsford, London, 1953.

Shakespeare's 'Measure for Measure', Mary Lascelles, London, 1953.

The First Night of 'Twelfth Night', Leslie Hotson, New York, 1954.

Shakespeare: The Last Phase, Derek Traversi, London, 1954.

Wise Fools in Shakespeare, R. H. Goldsmith, East Lansing, Mich., 1955; Liverpool, 1958.

Shakespeare and his Comedies, John Russell Brown, London, 1957, rev. 1962.

Shakespeare's Festive Comedy: A Study of Dramatic Form and its Relation to Social Custom, C. L. Barber, Princeton, N.J., 1959.

Shakespeare's Comedies, Bertrand Evans, Oxford, 1960.

Last Periods of Shakespeare, Racine, and Ibsen, Kenneth Muir, Liverpool, 1961.

Shakespeare's 'Merry Wives of Windsor', William Green, Princeton, N.J., 1962.

The Truth About Shylock, Bernard Grebanier, New York, 1962.

The Recurring Miracle: A Study of 'Cymbeline' and the Last Plays, D. R. C. Marsh, Durban, 1964.

Shakespeare's 'Troilus and Cressida' and its Setting, Robert Kimbrough, Cambridge, Mass., 1964.

A Natural Perspective: The Development of Shakespearean Comedy and Romance, Northrop Frye, New York, 1965.

On the Compositional Genetics of 'The Comedy of Errors', T. W. Baldwin, Urbana, Ill., 1965.

Shakespeare and the Comedy of Forgiveness, R. G. Hunter, New York, 1965.

Shakespeare's Early Comedies, E. M. W. Tillyard, London, 1965.

The Achievement of Shakespeare's 'Measure for Measure', David Lloyd Stevenson, New York, 1966.

Shakespeare's Romantic Comedies, Peter G. Phialas, Chapel Hill, N.C., 1966.

Something of Great Constancy: The Art of 'A Midsummer Night's Dream', David P. Young, New Haven, Conn., 1966.

Two Concepts of Allegory: A Study of Shakespeare's 'The Tempest' and the Logic of Allegorical Expression, A. D. Nuttall, London, 1967.

The Unfortunate Comedy: A Study of 'All's Well that Ends Well' and its Critics, Joseph G. Price, Toronto, 1968.

Shakespearian Comedy, ed. M. Bradbury and D. J. Palmer (Stratford-upon-Avon Studies 14), London, 1972.

Shakespeare and the Traditions of Comedy, L. G. Salingar, Cambridge, 1974.

Shakespeare's Comedy of Love, Alexander Leggatt, London, 1974.

13. CRITICAL STUDIES OF THE ENGLISH HISTORY PLAYS

An Essay on the Dramatic Character of Sir John Falstaff (1777), Maurice Morgann, in his *Shakespearian Criticism*, ed. D. A. Fineman, Oxford, 1972, etc.

Shakespeare's Hand in the Play of 'Sir Thomas More', ed. A. W. Pollard, Cambridge, 1923.

The Fortunes of Falstaff, J. Dover Wilson, Cambridge, 1943.

Shakespeare's History Plays, E. M. W. Tillyard, London, 1944.

Shakespeare's 'Histories': Mirrors of Elizabethan Policy, Lily B. Campbell, San Marino, Calif., 1947.

The English History Play in the Age of Shakespeare, Irving Ribner, Princeton, N.J., 1957; rev. London, 1965.
The Cease of Majesty: A Study of Shakespeare's History Plays, M. M. Reese, London, 1961.
Shakespeare's Histories: Plays for the Stage, Arthur Colby Sprague, London, 1964.
Shakespeare's Political Plays, H. M. Richmond, New York, 1967.
A Commentary on Shakespeare's 'Richard III', Wolfgang H. Clemen, London, 1968.
Divine Providence in the England of Shakespeare's Histories, H. A. Kelly, Cambridge, Mass., 1970.
Shakespeare's Heroical Histories: 'Henry VI' and its Literary Tradition, David Riggs, Cambridge, Mass., 1971.
A Kingdom for a Stage: The Achievement of Shakespeare's History Plays, Robert Ornstein, Cambridge, Mass., 1972.
The Drama of Power: Studies in Shakespeare's History Plays, Moody E. Prior, Evanston, Ill., 1973.
Patterns of Decay: Shakespeare's Early Histories, Edward I. Berry, Charlottesville, Va., 1975.

14. CRITICAL STUDIES OF THE TRAGEDIES AND ROMAN PLAYS

Shakespearean Tragedy, A. C. Bradley, London, 1904.
Shakespeare's Roman Plays and their Background, M. W. MacCallum, London, 1910.
Hamlet: An Historical and Comparative Study, Elmer Edgar Stoll, Minneapolis, Minn., 1919.
Shakespeare's Tragic Heroes: Slaves of Passion, Lily B. Campbell, Cambridge, 1930.
Hamlet: A Study in Critical Method, A. J. A. Waldock, Cambridge, 1931.
What Happens in 'Hamlet', J. Dover Wilson, Cambridge, 1935.
This Great Stage: Image and Structure in 'King Lear', Robert B. Heilman, Baton Rouge, La., 1948.
Shakespearian Tragedy, H. B. Charlton, Cambridge, 1948.
Hamlet and Oedipus, Ernest Jones, London, 1949.
Shakespeare's Doctrine of Nature: A Study of 'King Lear', John F. Danby, London, 1949.
The Royal Play of 'Macbeth', H. N. Paul, New York, 1950.
Shakespeare's Tragic Frontier, Willard Farnham, Berkeley, Calif., 1950.
The Dream of Learning: An Essay on 'The Advancement of Learning', 'Hamlet', and 'King Lear', D. G. James, Oxford, 1951.
Hamlet, Father and Son, Peter Alexander, Oxford, 1955.
Magic in the Web: Action and Language in 'Othello', Robert B. Heilman, Lexington, Ky., 1956.

Not Wisely but Too Well: Shakespeare's Love Tragedies, Franklin M. Dickey, San Marino, Calif., 1957.

The Structure of 'Julius Caesar', Adrien Bonjour, Liverpool, 1958.

Shakespeare and the Allegory of Evil: The History of a Metaphor in Relation to his Major Villains, Bernard Spivack, New York, 1958.

On the Design of Shakespearian Tragedy, H. S. Wilson, Toronto, 1959.

The Question of Hamlet, Harry Levin, New York, 1959.

An Approach to 'Hamlet', L. C. Knights, London, 1960.

Patterns in Shakespearian Tragedy, Irving Ribner, New York, 1960.

The Masks of Othello: The Search for the Identity of Othello, Iago, and Desdemona by Three Centuries of Actors and Critics, Marvin Rosenberg, Berkeley, Calif., 1961.

Shakespeare's Roman Plays: The Function of Imagery in the Drama, Maurice Charney, Cambridge, Mass., 1961.

The Story of the Night: Studies in Shakespeare's Major Tragedies, John Holloway, London, 1961.

'Hamlet' and the Philosophy of Literary Criticism, Morris Weitz, Chicago, Ill., 1965.

'King Lear' in Our Time, Maynard Mack, Berkeley, Calif., 1965.

King Lear and the Gods, William R. Elton, San Marino, Calif., 1966.

Fools of Time: Studies in Shakespearean Tragedy, Northrop Frye, Toronto, 1967.

Shakespeare's Early Tragedies, Nicholas Brooke, London, 1968.

Macbeth and the Players, Dennis Bartholomeusz, Cambridge, 1969.

Style in 'Hamlet', Maurice Charney, Princeton, N.J., 1969.

Hero and Saint: Shakespeare and the Graeco-Roman Tradition, Reuben A. Brower, Oxford, 1971.

Poison, Play, and Duel: A Study in 'Hamlet', Nigel Alexander, London, 1971.

The Masks of King Lear, Marvin Rosenberg, Berkeley, Calif., 1972.

Shakespeare's Tragic Sequence, Kenneth Muir, London, 1972.

Shakespeare: Seven Tragedies: The Dramatist's Manipulation of Response, E. A. J. Honigmann, London, 1976.

15. CRITICAL STUDIES OF THE POEMS AND SONNETS

The Sense of Shakespeare's Sonnets, Edward Hubler, Princeton, N.J., 1952.

The Mutual Flame: On Shakespeare's Sonnets and 'The Phoenix and the Turtle', G. Wilson Knight, London, 1955.

Themes and Variations in Shakespeare's Sonnets, J. B. Leishman, London, 1961.

The Shakespeare Sonnet Order, Brents Stirling, Berkeley, Calif., 1968.

An Essay on Shakespeare's Sonnets, Stephen Booth, New Haven, Conn., 1969.

Shakespeare's Dramatic Meditations, Giorgio Melchiori, Oxford, 1976.

16. RECORDINGS

The Marlowe Society of Cambridge, with professional players, has recorded the complete works under the direction of George Rylands in Dover Wilson's text for Argo. Most of the works have been recorded by professional players in G. B. Harrison's text on the Caedmon label. Other recordings of individual plays and extracts may be traced through the catalogues of the record companies.